D1563313

THE FATHERS SPEAK

THE FATHERS SPEAK

St Basil the Great
St Gregory of Nazianzus
St Gregory of Nyssa

Selected letters and life-records
translated from the Greek and introduced

by

GEORGES A. BARROIS

with a Foreword

by

JOHN MEYENDORFF

ST VLADIMIR'S SEMINARY PRESS
CRESTWOOD, NEW YORK 10707
1986

Library of Congress Cataloging-in-Publication Data

Main entry under title:

The Fathers speak, Saint Basil the Great, Saint Gregory of
    Nazianzus, Saint Gregory of Nyssa.

    1. Cappadocian Fathers—Correspondence. 2. Basil,
Saint, Bishop of Caesarea, ca. 329-379—Correspondence.
3. Gregory, of Nazianzus, Saint—Correspondence.
4. Gregory, of Nyssa, Saint, ca. 335-ca. 394—
Correspondence. I. Basil, Saint, Bishop of Caesarea, ca.
329-379. II. Gregory, of Nazianzus, Saint.
III. Gregory, of Nyssa, Saint, ca. 335-ca. 394.
IV. Barrois, George Augustin, 1898-
BR63.F28   1986   270.2   85-31958
ISBN 0-88141-037-3

BR
63
.B370
1986

THE FATHERS SPEAK

© Copyright 1986

by

ST VLADIMIR'S SEMINARY PRESS

ISBN 0-88141-037-3

PRINTED IN THE UNITED STATES OF AMERICA
BY
ATHENS PRINTING COMPANY
New York, NY 10018

In loving remembrance of
FATHER ALEXANDER SCHMEMANN
an intimate friend
of long years
Memory Eternal!

Contents

Contents

Foreword

As we Christians of the twentieth century study the Fathers of the Church, their writings—often, in an unreadable English produced by clumsy translators—appear to us as foreboding, verbose, and somewhat closed within a world where theological contemplation replaces everyday reality. The Greek Fathers in particular, have this reputation among students because they wrote relatively little about themselves, about the details of their own lives and the circumstances of daily life. Only St Augustine's *Confessions* have brought that author close to people of all cultures and all epochs.

Here for the first time is an anthology of texts by Greek authors, gathered almost exclusively from the personal correspondence between St Basil the Great, his close friend Gregory "the Theologian" and his younger brother Gregory of Nyssa. These three men appear to us as real human beings, reveal the substance of their Christian vocation, uncover the program of their spiritual life, unveil the intellectual background of their use of Greek philosophy at the service of Christian theology, and explain the meaning of their ministry as monastic leaders and bishops of the Church.

Readers of this book will be able to contemplate the icons of these Fathers in a new way, and with a fuller understanding of the human reality which appears iconographically transfigured in frescoes and mosaics. For indeed it is their genuinely human response to divine love and grace which has made them into "Holy Fathers," into saints of the Church.

This selection of texts and the commentary on them are the extraordinary achievement of a truly great scholar. With his unpretentious but remarkably thorough method of re-

9

search, Georges Barrois crowns his career as a Biblical archaeologist, Old Testament scholar and historian of medieval Latin thought with this work of spiritual devotion and ultimate commitment. The wisdom which the Fathers sought, which they have recognized fully in Jesus, the incarnate Logos, and which they never ceased to contemplate wherever they could discover it—in Plato, in the ascetic achievements of holy works, in nature and, indeed, in the divine image present in every human being—permeates this book.

This Wisdom is indeed "manifold" (πολυποίκιλος, Eph 3:10), and no one could have recognized it in the Fathers, still young men when they wrote these letters, better than the great and wise elder, Georges Barrois.

— *John Meyendorff*

Introduction

I am not writing a book about *the "Three Hierarchs," Saint Basil, Saint Gregory of Nazianzus, and Saint Gregory of Nyssa. I prefer to let them speak for themselves in the letters which they wrote to each other or to some of their contemporaries, and which let us enter into their intimacy. My task has been to choose those pieces that can best reveal the secret of their personality.*

I have made use of the following sources: For the letters of Saint Basil, the Greek text established by Yves Courtonne for the Collection Budé, *tome 1, Paris 1957; tome 2 (1961); and tome 3 (1966). For the letters of Saint Gregory of Nazianzus, the Greek text of Paul Gallay,* Collection Budé, *tome 1, Paris 1964, and tome 2 (1967). One will regret the complicated apparatus of footnotes and supplementary remarks at the end of each volume.*

The thirty-three letters of Saint Gregory of Nyssa pose a special problem: the manuscripts and the early printed editions attribute some of these letters confusedly to Gregory of Nazianzus or to Gregory of Nyssa, and even to Basil. The difficulty is compounded with the fact that the Gregorii Nysseni epistulae *in the Jaeger edition of the* Opera Omnia *(volume 3:2), were copyrighted by E. J. Brill (Leiden, 1959), but the origin of this edition of the* epistulae *antecedes the volumes of the Budé collection, with a series of unforeseen and unfortunate circumstances (war, a broken leg, and a severe illness) having delayed the inclusion of the Florentine scholar Giorgio Pasquali's remarkable analysis of the manuscripts in the Jaeger edition.*

I have used for my selections from the Life of Moses *the text of the late Cardinal Daniélou,* Sources Chrétiennes,

vol. 1 bis, Paris, 1955, and for those from the Life of Saint
Macrina *the text published by Pierre Maraval in the same
collection, vol. 178, Paris, 1971. Needless to say, my English
rendering is not a translation from the French versions, but
from the original Greek.*

*I regret that I was not able to achieve a complete uni-
formity in the rendering of the names of persons or of places,
since some have been consecrated by English usage and some
have been Latinized, while others call for a mere transcription of the Greek form. Nor have I been able to achieve
consistency in capitalizing some formulae like "Your Honor,"
"Your Piety," "Your Prudence," and the like, lavished by
our hierarchs on their correspondents. Are they uniformly
part of the Byzantine protocol, or are they meant as free
compliments? It is at times hard to decide.*

*I have met repeatedly, in the course of my reading, the
words* philosophy, philosopher, philosophize, *and the like.
They may, and do, mean rather different things, for example,
the academic discipline that Basil and Gregory of Nazianzus
had acquired in Athens; or is there meant by* philosophizing
*an exchange of opinions among friends commenting on world
events in which they claim to be totally un-engaged? Or is*
philosophy *to be understood as Christian wisdom, a Christian's ordering of his own life in the light of faith? The con-
text of the letters alone will be our surest guide in these matters. (See the remarkable étude of Anne-Marie Malingrey,*
"Philosophia," Etude d'un groupe de mots dans la litterature
grecque, des Présocratiques au IVème siècle après Jésus
Christ, *Paris, 1961.)*

*I have avoided the use of footnotes, used—and abused—
in such pieces of writing as theses, but my book is emphati-
cally not a thesis. Whenever necessary, I have introduced a
few words of explanation, in square brackets, into the text
of the selections.*

*Let me remind my readers that the selections I offer are
the essential feature of this book and that my own comments
are meant as mere guides for making the thought of the
Three Hierarchs more accessible to our contemporaries.*

On the point of closing this general introduction, I want

to express my thanks to all those who have manifested some interest in my work; it was for me a precious encouragement. My wife, Dr. Augusta V. Barrois, has typed my long-hand first draft of the manuscript—no mean task!—and helped me straighten up my English in the course of daily sessions, at times stormy, but always a labor of love undertaken with a professional understanding of the historical realities.

1

The Solitude in Pontus

We begin our pilgrimage in the wooded solitude of Annisi (Ἀννήσοι) in Pontus, cradle of Basilian monasticism, where the founder and hegumen of a community of monks and religious women, having been called—not by his choice—to the metropolitan see of Caesaraea in Cappadocia, returned home whenever a lull in the affairs of his Church procured him a too rare but most welcome occasion.

Here is Basil's own description of the solitude, to which he hoped to attract his friend Gregory of Nazianzus, his condisciple at the schools of Athens. In this he was unsuccessful. Gregory loved Basil dearly, but he did not like the place; hence, a lively exchange of sour-sweet letters between the two friends.

The description is meant to give us an idea of the place, with an overload of poetic and mythological allusions; after all, one has been to Athens, and one is eager to show it off: the island of Calypso; the Strymon, a river in Thracia, made famous by the wars of Alexander; the Echinades, islands of the Ionian Sea where Alkmaion, pursued by the Furies, attempted to find refuge. Basil relished these clichés, and Gregory found in them a ready aliment for the devastating irony of his letters to his friend, dated from the early years of the community at Annisi. It would be futile, on the sole basis of Basil's description, to attempt an objective reconstitution of the solitude and of the monastic settlement.

BASIL, LETTER 14, TO HIS FRIEND GREGORY OF NAZIANZUS
(written after 360 but before 364)

... I had set out for Pontus in search of a way of life,
and God did show me a place that suits perfectly my mood.
... It is a high mountain covered with a dense forest, irri-
gated on the north side by cool and limpid waters. At its
foot stretches an inclined plain fertilized by the water that
drips continually from the mountain. Woods have grown
spontaneously around the plain, various trees of all kinds
forming almost a sort of hedge. The island of Calypso, which
Homer admired above all others for its beauty, is small in
comparison. Our place is not far from being an island, for
it is isolated on either side by deep ravines. On the flank of
the mountain, the steep banks of the river form a continuous,
impassable wall. The mountain extends on both sides, crescent-shaped, along the contour of the ravines, thus ruling
out any access to flat grounds; there is only one passage,
which we control. Another dale below the crest near the
main summit of the mountain shelters our home, so that the
plain below extends under our eyes; from up there, one can
even see the river below, as it circles the entire area. The
river is no less enjoyable, so it seems to me, than the Strymon
as seen from Amphipolis in Thracia. The Strymon flows
slowly and ends in a swamp; it ceases almost to be a river,
so sluggish it becomes; but our brook runs faster than any
of the rivers I know; its wild waters rush from under the
rocks nearby, gush forth and roll into a deep whirlpool.
The view gives me much pleasure, as it does to all sightseers.
It is equally precious to all the inhabitants of the region for
the incredible abundance of fish which feed in the eddies.
And shall we mention the fragrance arising from the earth,
or the breeze from the river? Let another wonder at the
multitude of flowers and singing birds; I am not at leisure
to apply my mind to it. The most I can say of this land is
that it is ready to bear all sorts of fruit on account of its
favorable location. It feeds me with the most delectable

fruit—quietude—and not only because it does not allow wanderers, except the hunters who come to us; for among other advantages, our land is rich in game, not your bears or wolves, God forbid, but herds of deer, wild goats, grazing hares, and similar beasts. Think a while the risk I would incur if by stupidity I would exchange such a land for the Tibernene [the region of Nazianzus], refuse pit [βάραθρον] of the universe! Forgive my hurry to go home. Neither did Alkmaion continue his wandering, after he had found the Echinades.

Gregory failed to appreciate the charms of the solitude in Pontus, and Basil hated the harsh climate of Nazianzus and the Tibernene, its winter rains, its muddy roads, a quagmire, the "refuse pit of the universe." Little wonder that Gregory felt hurt! The two friends, all their life long, had had their measure of personal disagreements. This time, they vented their difference half in jest, half in earnest.

Paul Gallay, the editor of Gregory's letters, thought that when letter II was written, Basil, the addressee, was still traveling and not yet settled at Annisi. Basil's letter 14, containing the offensive allusions to the Tibernene, would have been preceded by another letter, presumably lost or unrecorded. Is this hypothesis necessary? We might credit Basil with enough common sense and tact not to repeat his derogative comments, and we prefer to regard Gregory's letter 2 as a straight reply to Basil's letter 14.

Gregory sees irony in Basil's improbable luxury in the course of his peregrinations in quest of models of spiritual life among Eastern and Egyptian monastics and anchorites. The random inns of the traveler are magnified comically as palaces—the Hiltons and Hyatts of the time—and Basil's earnest search is decried as loafing on the agora. The exchange of lampoons continued for quite some time, until the two friends agreed to bury the hatchet. The charms of the Pontic solitude for which Gregory showed little appreciation would be his next target.

GREGORY OF NAZIANZUS, LETTER 2,
TO BASIL (361)

I cannot bear that you decry the Tibernene, its mud and
its winter rains; oh you who have no mud and go tip-toeing
on parquet floors; you the airborne man who flies on the dart
of Abaris [a mythological hero who was said to ride on the
arrows of Apollo]! You, a Cappadocian, who run away from
Cappadocia! Is it our fault if you are pallid, confined without
breathing space, and if the sun is meagerly measured to you?
Meanwhile you say that we are fat, replete, bursting with
health, and you are not! We are supposed to have pleasure,
abundance, and to loaf about the agora! No, I won't buy
that! And stop reproaching us our mud. You have not
created your city [Caesaraea, birthplace of Basil], nor are
we responsible for our winter rains. Or else I am going to
balance our mud [πηλῶν] with your taverns [καπηλούς]
and all the evils which your cities bring about!

GREGORY OF NAZIANZUS, LETTER 4, TO BASIL (361)

Deride and criticize our place, in jest or in earnest!
That's nothing. Only smile, have your fill of culture, and
enjoy our friendship. Coming from you, all this gives us
pleasure, whatever it is and however it is. . . . As for me, I
am going to admire your Pontus, your Pontic lair and your
solitude, a worthy place of exile: these mountain ridges
above your heads, those wild beasts which put your faith to
test, that plain extending below, and even your rat hole with
its pompous labels: φροντιστήριον [cf. Socrates' "thinking
shop"]; μοναστήριον, monastery [a neologism in Gregory's
time]; σχολή, school! And what of those thickets and wild

woods, that crown of mountainous cliffs which does not crown, but rather hems you in. . . . I also praise the way "strait and narrow" [Mt 7:14]; I know not whether it leads into the Kingdom or into Hades—admittedly, for your sake, into the Kingdom! And in the midst of it all, what do you want me to say? . . . Everything that is not rock is ravine, everything that is not ravine is brambles, and all that are not brambles are overhanging cliffs. The path climbs up in overhang and is precipitous on all sides; it besets the spirits of the travelers and forces them into acrobatics for their own safety. A stream runs below; it is for you the Strymon of Amphipolis, which is so calm, but your stream is richer in pebbles than in fish, nor does it empty into a lake, but rushes down into an abyss, oh you lover of high-sounding words and maker of neologisms. It is enormous, that stream, terrible, more loud than the psalmody up there. The waterfalls and cataracts of the Nile are nothing in comparison, so much it bellows against you day and night; fierce, it cannot be crossed; muddy, its water is undrinkable; all its humaneness consists in that it does not sweep your house away, when torrents and tempests rage in winter. That is what we feel about your "Islands of the Blessed" [ancient heroes], rather the islands of blessed you! And now, admire the crescent-shaped heights which choke rather than protect your slopes, and the rim that extends above you; it makes you a life of Tantalus! And the winds that blow through, and the fragrance of the earth which revives you when you feel downhearted! And the singing birds that sing a song of famine and fly over a desert! "Nobody comes," you say, "except in the hunting season." Add this: "and to visit the dead that we are"! My chatter is too long for a letter, yet still shorter than a comedy. If you can take the joke, good; but if not, we will add a few more.

GREGORY OF NAZIANZUS, LETTER 5, TO BASIL (361)

Since you take jokes as you ought to, I am going to add these: My preamble shall be from Homer. Go one and sing the beautiful indoors, the roofless and doorless hovel, the chimney with neither flame nor smoke; the walls let to dry by the fire, lest we be smirched with mud; the miserable and meager banquet to which we were invited from Cappadocia, not as to the frugal breakfast of the Lotophagi, but as to the sumptuous table of Alkinoüs, poor shipwrecked we! I remember your breads and your soups—that is what you call those! I remember our teeth grinding on the crust, getting stuck as in putty—we could not get them loose! Now you are going to overdramatize it all, finding in whatever you endure a pretext for raising your voice! If that great foster mother of the poor, I mean your mother, had not hurried to rescue us at the right moment, like a haven unto storm-beaten travelers, we would be long since nothing but corpses, and our "Pontic faith" [proverbial locution: a faith "not to be trusted"] would call for less praise than pity! . . . If you are not hurt by what I say, I feel not hurt either; but let us forget whatever we went through, and draw some profit from it.

The worst of the quarrel between Basil and Gregory was over. The letters from Nazianzus that follow are more irenic, but mildly ironic. Gregory, who had also his "solitude" in the family estate at Arianzus, was conscious of having forced the jeering note; now (letter 6), he recants. In spite of his lack of appreciation for the site of Annisi, he had made, or would make, visits or longer sojourns at the community center.

GREGORY OF NAZIANZUS, LETTER 6, TO BASIL (361)

Whatever we wrote to you about the Pontic way of life was in jest, not in earnest. But what I am writing now is very serious. "Who shall give me to be like in the months of yore" [Jb 29:2], when together with you I made suffering my delight, since pain willingly endured is more precious than unwelcome pleasure. Who shall give us these psalmodies, these vigils, these raptures toward God in prayer, and that life beyond the world of matter and beyond the body, so to speak? That togetherness and communion with the brethren, being "deified" [θεουμένων], and lifted up through you? And what about that emulation and eagerness for virtue, which we have made secure through written rules and canons? What of our labor of love for the divine words, and the light we discovered in them under the guidance of the Spirit? Or, to speak of smaller and lesser things, what of the daily chores and the toil of our hands: the timber, the quarrying of building stones, the gardens to be watered, and the plane-tree, a golden plane-tree more precious than that of Xerxes [Herodotus VII, 31]. It is not an effeminate king who sat in its shade. Our tree, "I planted it; Apollos . . ."—that means you, O excellent Basil—"Apollos watered it, and God gave it to grow" [1 Co 3:6], all for our sake, that the remembrance of our labor may subsist among you, as it is said that the wand of Aaron budded in the Ark [Nb 17:8-10]. Praying for all this is easy, but to realize it is difficult. Stand by me, that together we breathe and cultivate virtue; whatever we harvest, may we preserve it through prayer, lest we faint, little by little, like a shadow at the passing of day. I breathe you more than I breathe air; I live only when I am with you, or, either present or absent, through remembrance.

2
Biographicals

It would be much to say that the descriptions of the "solitude" in Pontus and the saucy comments of Gregory of Nazianzus make us visualize the landscape of Annisi. We can at least imagine what it looked like: the wooded hills, the precipitous cliffs, the underlying meadows, the sinuous course of the Iris and the brooks tumbling down from the crags of the mountain, obviously a site fit for cenobites and hermits eager to flee the "world," but not the elaborate monasteries of the Athos or the forbidding stone-pillars of the Meteora; rather, an agglomeration of shanties akin to those of Saint Francis and his early disciples in the gorge of the Carceri, where they fished—or poached?—the brook trout of the Abbot of Monte Subasio. Now, who were the solitaries? Let us identify a few of them and let the letters of Basil and Gregory of Nazianzus introduce them to us.

Saint Basil the Great was born in Caesaraea of Cappadocia (Kayseri), the country of his mother, around 329-330. He attended local schools and struck a lasting friendship (not exempt of piques!) with Gregory of Nazianzus, whom he accompanied to study—unhurriedly—in Athens. He was supposed to prepare himself for the profession of rhetor. On their return from Greece, he parted from his companion and took to extensive traveling through the entire Middle East (358-359), eager to acquaint himself with groups of men and women living in the observance of the precepts and the counsels of the Evangel, or retiring into the "desert" as anchorites. Back in Pontus, he founded the communal center of Christian living at Annisi on the Iris (the Yesil

Irmak). Ordained to the priesthood as a hieromonk by Eusebius of Caesaraea, he succeeded him on the first see of Cappadocia, in 370. He died in his charge on the first of January 379.

Basil had hoped for a time that Gregory, his companion of the Athenian years, would join him in the solitude of Annisi. But Gregory, who had to take care of his aging parents, could not accept the invitation. That was a valid and honest excuse; besides, Gregory did not share Basil's infatuation with the site. Thus he wrote to Basil:

GREGORY OF NAZIANZUS TO BASIL, LETTER 1 (361)

I failed to be with you and philosophize with you, after we had pledged, in our Athenian days, friendship and "growth into one" [συμφυία]—I do not find a more fitting word! But if I have failed, it is unwillingly. A law prevailed over another law: the law of taking care of my parents, over the law of comradeship and togetherness. But I shall not fail altogether if you agree on this, that I be sometime with you, and do consent to be sometime with us in Nazianzus; so we would have everything in common, and in conformity with our friendship. In that way it will be easy not to grieve my parents, and still to meet with you.

GREGORY OF NAZIANZUS TO BASIL, LETTER 60 (372-373)

. . . We are at the bedside of our lady mother, who has been afflicted with illness for a long time. Were it not that we ought not to leave her in that critical condition, we would not penalize ourselves by not coming to you, be assured of it. Only, do help her through your prayers for her health, and for assisting us in our journey.

In the interval between these two letters, Gregory had visited Basil at Annisi on several occasions, once the pique that had nearly wrecked the friendship of the two ex-Athenians was over and the concord restored.

Basil's family formed the core of the community of Annisi. On his father's side he could claim the eastern part of Pontus as his home. His father (died ca. 341) was a rhetor at Neo-Caesaraea (Niksar), and pleaded before the imperial courts of law. In Basil's advanced years, the city was dissurbed by factions, and his personal reputation as well as his orthodoxy were challenged by Atarbios, the bishop, whom he reported to be the originator of those nonsensical rumors. Basil countered by reminding the Neo-Caesaraeans of his own ancestry, thus making improbable the accusations of his enemies, unless he would have totally forfeited his forebears—an inconceivability!—(letters 204 and 210).

Basil to the People of Neo-Caesaraea, through their Priests, Letter 204 (375)

. . . If the fact of having the same teachers contributes greatly to union, we have had with you the same masters to teach us the divine mysteries, and the same spiritual fathers who from the beginning founded your Church. I mean Gregory the Wonderworker [died ca. 270] and all who, rising like stars, marched in his footsteps and left manifest signs for living unto heaven to all who are willing. If natural kinship is not negligible, and contributes mightily to unbreakable union and fellowship of life, here again we have some rights toward you. . . . Could there be a clearer test of our faith than that we have been brought up by a blessed grandmother from your midst? I mean the distinguished Macrina, who taught us the words of the blessed Gregory the Wonderworker, guided as she was by the remembrance of his sayings, retaining them for herself and unto the education and formation of the tiny child I was at that time in the doctrines of piety. When we came to the age of discernment and were given to reach maturity, we wandered over many lands and seas, following the men whom we might find addicted to the rule of pious living, and we counted them as our fathers and guides of our soul in the road that leads to God.

BASIL TO THE LEADING CITIZENS OF NEO-CAESARAEA (λογιωτάτοις), LETTER 210 (375)

I felt absolutely no need to broadcast my thoughts, nor to tell you why I am actually in these parts, for I do not wish to make a show of myself, nor does the present affair warrant so many witnesses! I realize we do not do what we wish, but what your leaders incite us to do, for I have more zeal to stay utterly unnoticed than your glory-seekers display to shine. As I hear, all the people in your city have their ears worn out, and there are makers of high tales, workers of falsehood, hired to the very purpose of telling you all about me. I do not think that I should overlook your indoctrination by evil-minded and foul talkers, but rather explain myself. From childhood on I have been at home in this region, where I was brought up by my grandmother [Macrina the elder] and where I sojourned a great deal since, trying to flee political turmoil. I realized that these parts were favorable to "philosophizing," for the solitary quietude in which I passed several years at a stretch, and in which my brothers live now. This is why, catching a breathing spell in the midst of the occupations that detain us, I was glad to come to this retreat, not to cause trouble to others, but rather to satisfy my own desire. . . .

What need is there to resort to visions, to hire interpreters of dreams, and to make us a drunken tale in public banquets? If I had been calumniated by other people, it is you whom I would have called upon to witness to my dispositions. And now I ask from everyone to remember the old days when the city entrusted us with its youth, when men in authority were sent to us as a deputation, and how the entire people in a body surrounded us. What did they not give? What did they not promise? Yet they could not retain us. How then, after declining the invitation, would I enter by force now that I am not invited? How, as I run away from my supporters and admirers, would I come now to pursue my slanderers?

We may draw up now the list of Basil's brothers and sisters, born to mother Emmelia, as follows:

Saint Macrina the younger, born c. 327, died late 379.

Saint Basil "the Great," born c. 329, archbishop of Caesaraea (370), died on January 1, 379.

Naukratios, born c. 330, an anchorite, died accidentally c. 357.

Saint Gregory of Nyssa, born c. 340, died 394.

Peter, the last child of Emmelia, (345-392), ordained a priest around 371-375, in charge of the men at Annisi. He became bishop of Sebastaea (Sivas) in

*Lesser Armenia, when his brother Gregory, who had
been exiled by order of Valens, was able to return to
Nyssa.*

*We know close to nothing of two more sisters of Basil;
the existence of an eighth child of Emmelia, a certain Nike-
phoros, is highly problematic. We have followed in this list
the dates given, mostly in footnotes, by P. Maraval, in his
edition of the* Vie de Sainte Macrine, *(Sources Chrétiennes,
vol. 178, Paris 1971).*

We conclude this section by excerpting from the Life of
Saint Macrina *a fragment on the tragic death of Naukratios;
in spite of a note of artificiality observed by Maraval and
A.M. Festugière, the relation is exceptionally realistic and
the effects of style, common to the hagiography of the time,
are reduced to a minimum.*

GREGORY OF NYSSA, LIFE OF SAINT MACRINA:
THE DEATH OF NAUKRATIOS
[*Sources Chrétiennes*, vol. 178, sections 8-10]

. . . Moved by a divine foresight, Naukratios despised all
he possessed and, under a mighty impulse of spirit, converted
to a solitary life of poverty, taking with him naught but
himself. One of his house servants, Chrysaphios by name,
followed him, both out of personal attachment and because
he had decided to adopt the same way of life. Naukratios
lived by himself, in a retreat he had discovered near the Iris.
The Iris is a river that flows through the Pontus; it has its
source in Armenia, flows through our regions, and empties
into the *Pontus Euxinus* [the Black Sea]. Along the river,
the young man found a place covered by a dense forest, hidden in a rocky hollow of the mountain ridge. He dwelt there,
far from the hubbub of the city and from the contentions and

struggles of courtroom rhetorics. Having delivered himself of all the echoes of human life, he nursed with his own hands some old people, sick and destitute, thinking that such activity suited his way of life. Being handy in all the arts of hunting, he used to go on the hunt, thus providing the old people with food, and he subdued his youthfulness by the fatigues of the hunt. And he conformed himself eagerly to the will of his mother [Emmelia] if she would demand something from him. Thus he organized his life in two ways: mastering his own youth by hard work, and being guided, through his mother's zeal, in the observance of the divine precepts.

For five years he lived in that manner, "philosophizing" and giving joy to his mother by his own way of life, since he ordered his life through temperance, and fulfilled with all his power the wishes of her who had borne him. But then a heavy and tragic blow, a machination, methinks, of the Adversary [the Devil], afflicted the mother, and it was such that it affected the entire family with grief and mourning. All of a sudden Naukratios was torn away from life; no illness had provoked this misfortune; no ordinary or trivial causes had brought about the death of the young man. One day he went hunting, so that he could provide for the necessities of the old people in his hospice. And he was carried back home, dead, and with him his companion Chrysaphios! The mother was away, far from the tragic event, when a messenger brought her the news.

More details on the accidental death of Naukratios are found in an epitaphion *by St Gregory of Nazianzus (Migne P.G. 38, 11 A). Naukratios and his companion were drowned while trying to disentangle their dragnet caught in the rocks at the bottom of the turbulent Iris. Note that* θήρα, θηράω, *normally "hunting," can also mean "fishing." Cf. Plato,* Leges *823d: "sea-fishing"; Aristophanes, 864: "fishing for eels."*

*A journey of some 200 miles southeast of Neo-Caesaraea
in Pontus would lead us through Cappadocia to the region
of Nazianzus, the Tibernene, odious to Basil on account of
its harsh winter rains, but the fatherland of Gregory, who was
born in 329-330 at Arianzus, a suburb of Nazianzus, where
his family owned the domain of Kerbela. The father,
Gregory the elder, was a convert from the sect of Hypsis-
tarians, who worshiped the "God Most High," El-'Elyôn,
Θεὸς "Υψιστος, and kept some judaizing observances.
Gregory the elder became bishop of Nazianzus in 329. The
mother, Nonna, was a native of Caesaraea, a Christian from
childhood. After a sojourn of several years in Athens, where
he studied together with Basil, Gregory returned directly to
Nazianzus (358-359), and was ordained to the priesthood
by his father (ca. 361-362), whom he assisted in the work
of the Church. Shortly before Easter 372, Gregory was
consecrated bishop of Sasima, but found his see usurped by
the intrigant Anthimios; he remained provisionally as auxil-
iary bishop to his aging father, who died in 374.*

*The contrast between the life of the solitaries in Pontus
and the household at Arianzus is striking: on the banks of
the Iris, a monastic center; at Arianzus, a lively family life.
Kaisarios, Gregory's younger brother, went to study medi-
cine in Alexandria, and eventually became in Constantinople
the physican "à la mode." Gregory addressed to him a
severe letter (letter 7) prompted by the gossip of parishioners,
who had some pain understanding that the free ways of a
medic and the sense of propriety of small-town burghers
are seldom compatible.*

GREGORY OF NAZIANZUS TO KAISARIOS, HIS YOUNGER
BROTHER, LETTER 7 (362)

We have blushed and are much distressed about you. Do

we need to write to him who, more than anyone else, is himself aware of it? Without speaking of ourselves, of the sadness that bears on us, nor—let me say this—of the rumors one hears about you, I wish, if it is possible, that you would become aware of what others say about you and about us; not only our friends, but strangers as well, inasmuch as they are Christians. It is not just one or the other who talks; all are telling the same things, for men are more inclined to philosophizing about the affairs of their neighbors than about their own. This gossip has become just another exercise of rhetoric: "Now the son of a bishop has been enrolled into the imperial service; now he aspires to wordly power and glory; now he lets himself succumb to the lure of wealth, whereas the fire is kindled for all, and our souls are put in jeopardy." . . . Our noble father, much distraught by what he hears, is weary of life itself. I console and comfort him in whatever manner I can, vouching for your dispositions and persuading him that you shall not disappoint him any longer. Our lady mother, if she would hear anything about you—till now we have kept it hidden from her through many devices—she would conceive a pain inconsolable, because of feminine faintheartedness and also because of her excessive piety, which is incapable of moderation in such matters. If you prize yourself and ourselves highly enough, take some better and safer resolutions. Things around here are quite sufficient to insure a honest independence, provided one is not insatiable or immoderate by craving for more. If you wish to establish yourself, I do not see why you should delay more and let pass the propitious time. But if you persist in your state of mind—I do not want to tell you unpleasant things—I predict and I protest that you will be necessarily confronted with a dilemma: either, by remaining a true Christian, you will take place in a despised rank unworthy of yourself and of your hopes; or, by coveting honors, you will be harmed in what is essential, and suffer smoke if not even fire [cf. 1 Co 3:15].

Gregory had to take care of a goodly number of nephews and nieces, children of his sister Gorgonia. He undertook to guide these youngsters in life, and recommended them frequently to the attention of authorities, civil and religious. Here are a few samples.

The addressee of letter 14 is not to be identified with Kaisarios the physician, but a magistrate in Cappadocia. The "noble cousins" of whom Gregory is speaking are Helladios, who died in 372, and Eulalios, who was consecrated to the see of Nazianzus in 383. By that time Gregory had already retired to the family estate.

GREGORY OF NAZIANZUS TO KAISARIOS, A MAGISTRATE,
LETTER 14 (written before 372)

Grant yourself a favor; it is not one you will have to grant very often, for it does not happen often that such an occasion presents itself. Let the protection of an eminent act of justice protect my noble cousins, who are in trouble concerning some piece of real estate which they purchased to be a place of retirement and from which they might draw their subsistence. After closing the deed, they fell into various annoyances: dealing with a dishonest selling party, and also the damage and ravage caused by the neighbors. It might be advantageous for them to recover the money they gave in payment, together with the other expenses—not a mean sum—and to revoke the deal. Be good enough to have this affair deferred to you, so that the contract be drafted to the best advantage, after you will have examined the affair. This would be the most pleasant solution for them and for us. Otherwise, and this is my second request, stand up against the underhanded maneuvers and practices of that cheat [the seller]. By no means should he prevail over them and cause them a loss, whether they keep the property or revoke the sale.

Personally, I would blush from writing to you about such things. But we find ourselves under obligation to them, either because of our kinship, or because of the way of life they have chosen. Should we not take a special care for these men and blush with shame, and blush still more if we show no zeal to grant them these services? Anyway, whether for yourself, or for us, or for the cousins, or all these reasons together, be kind to them!

Gregory, having resigned his see of Constantinople by the leave of Emperor Theodosius, returned to his native Anatolia, where his fellow-bishops debated—acrimoniously, so it seems—what should be his canonical status. Gregory's personal decision to go into retirement thwarted their argumentative itch. Having lavished his biting irony on his colleagues, Gregory came to what was the real object of his letter: the children of his nephew Nikoboulos were being sent by their parents to study tachygraphy in the town of Tyana. Would Bishop Theodoros keep a discreet eye on them and see to it that they behave as good church-goers and God-fearing Christians. Tachygraphy, a sort of stenography, was commonly used for the recording of oral arguments in courts of law and agencies of government.

GREGORY OF NAZIANZUS TO THEODOROS,
BISHOP OF TYANA, LETTER 157
(Autumn 381 or Early 382)

. . . Finished with the spiritual concerns! I will not continue bothering you. Huddle ye together, fence yourselves in, and take counsel on our status! Let our adversaries be victorious, let them apply rigorously the canons, to begin with regard to me, who am stupid in those matters. I bear no grudge to rigorism [ἀκριβεία, in opposition to κατ' οἰκονομίαν], but let there be no hindrance to friendship! The children of our most esteemed "son" Nikoboulos have left for your town in order to learn tachygraphy. In general have an eye on them, kindly and fatherly—canons do not forbid that—and in particular see to it that they frequent the church. I wish that they form their character to virtue by following the example of Your Perfection.

It appears from this letter to Eudoxios, a Cappadocian rhetor to whom young Nikoboulos had been recommended by Gregory, that he was, like many gifted students, too easily satisfied with his own achievements and in need of a stricter discipline to give his full measure. Gregory illustrates his note with a quotation—rather far-fetched—of the legend of Eunomios the Lokrian at the Isthmian Games. A string of his lyre had snapped in the middle of an ode; a cicada, flying unto the yoke of the instrument, completed the interrupted chant with her own heavenly melody (cf. St Clement of Alexandria, Protreptikos I, 1, 2).

GREGORY OF NAZIANZUS TO EUDOXIOS, LETTER 175 (383)

My dear Nikoboulos goes to you again, and again I need not urge you, who are already eager by yourself. But because our young man has an instinctive facility—if my wishes do not deceive me—yet, this quality being allied to a certain negligence, as it frequently happens, he needs to be spurred on; do supply him with your own diligence! If I may use one of your sayings, imitate the cicada of the legend, replace for your Eunomios the broken string of his lyre, and complete the ode. I think this youngster will do you honor and will do us the greatest favor, to us who do not place many things above you and your talent.

GREGORY OF NAZIANZUS TO NIKOBOULOS, LETTER 51
(Date Uncertain)

This mini-treatise on the art of letter-writing is addressed to Nikoboulos, the elder and nephew-of-sorts of Gregory, who always took much interest in the numerous descendants of his sisters. Nikoboulos is a young man, apparently gifted, who had asked his uncle for advice. The dating of letter 51 fluctuates between 384 and 390 (Gallay). I have made a few cuts, at the risk of missing literary allusions or rhetorical flowers which might have been enjoyed by Hellenes—or Philhellenes—but would be lost on today's average readers.

The "Persian arpent" mentioned in letter 51 is a measure of length equal to ca. 700 feet. A "child's cubit" is measured from the elbow to the tip of the middle finger.

. . . Among those who write letters—since you question me on that subject—some write more than they should, and some not enough; neither of these keep the right measure, like bowmen shooting their arrows too far or too short, and they miss the target for contrary reasons. The proper measure in letter-writing is what the subject demands: one should not write at length if there is little to say, or niggardly if there is much matter. Then what? Shall we measure our wisdom by Persian arpents, or by a child's cubit? Either lack of measure should be avoided, in order to attain the right mean. That is what I think concerning brevity.

. . . About clarity, one should know this: flee oratoricals by all means, but incline rather toward the style of conversation. To say it in short, the best and perfect letter is the one that convinces the common man and the intellectual as well: the common man will know that it is on the level of everyone; the intellectual, that it is above the common. It should also be grasped right away. A letter that is dark like a riddle is as undesirable as one that needs a commentary.

. . . The third quality of a letter is grace. We secure this if our manner of writing is never dry, unpleasant, or awkward; never destitute of all charm, untidy, they would say: never devoid of maxims, proverbs, examples; not without those barbs which make a letter challenging; but we never must abuse of such finery. The former manner in the manner of a boor, the latter, that of a never satiated sophisticate.

. . . The conclusion I owe to one who said elegantly speaking of the eagles: When the birds contended for kingship and rivaled among themselves for being held most beautiful of all, the beauty of the eagle was precisely that he did not know he was beautiful. And here is what we much watch above all when we write letters: shun all affectation, and cling as much as we can to what is natural.

From Nazianzus, where he refused repeatedly to become the successor of his father, Gregory was called to take care of a little church frequented by the Orthodox minority in Constantinople. After the defeat of Valens in Thracia, his successor Theodosius, favorable to the Nicene party, elevated the church of the capital to patriarchal rank, a decision ratified by the First Council of Constantinople (381). Of poor health, however, Gregory resigned his charge and retired to Arianzus where he died in 390.

Most of the data relative to Gregory of Nyssa have

already been presented in the biographical notices on Saint Basil and Saint Gregory of Nazianzus. This younger brother of Saint Basil was born around 345 (see the discussion in Maraval, Vie de Sainte Macrina, *p. 48, note 2), presumably at Neo--Caesaraea in Pontus. He had planned, or it had been planned for him, that he would become a lawyer, but he joined the rest of the family in the community of Annisi. He was ordained to the priesthood in 362. The profile of Saint Gregory of Nyssa is quite different from that of his brother Basil and their friend from Nazianzus. He was married, which is the normal thing for an Orthodox priest. He appears to have been, his life long, an independent spirit, a philosopher, and a mystic. The following letter of Gregory of Nazianzus reproaches him for his mundane nature which was commented upon without indulgence by parishioners more used to the conventional manners of their clergy, and warns him against the neglect of the Holy Scriptures. This letter seems to have been written after his ordination to the priesthood and before his consecration as bishop of Nyssa.*

GREGORY OF NAZIANZUS TO GREGORY, THE FUTURE
BISHOP OF NYSSA, LETTER 11 (Date Uncertain)

. . . Why should you not hear from us, openly, that which they all whisper? They do not praise your glory ingloriously, if I may use one of your maxims, nor your giving way little by little, nor your love of honors—the worst of daemons, says Euripides [Phen 531-532]. What has befallen you, O most wise, and how can you endure reproaching yourself with having pushed aside the sacred books rich in sap, which you used to read publicly to the people [as a tonsured reader, ἀναγνώστης]? Are you not ashamed to hear this? Or did you put them away on the mantlepiece of your smoke-black-ened fireplace, like paddles or mattocks during the winter months? Instead, you have taken in hand dried-up, insipid writings, and the name of rhetor is more pleasant to your ear than the name of Christian. But we prefer the latter, and all thanks be to God! No my dear, do not suffer this any longer; sober up at last, come back into yourself, defend us before the faithful, defend yourself before God and before the mysteries from which you have estranged yourself! And do not serve me captious arguments in the manner of rhetors, saying: "What then? Was I not a Christian, while I was a rhetor?" No, my dear, you were not! Forgive if I make you sad, it is out of friendship; or if I flare up for your own good, the good of the entire priestly order and, I should add, of all Christians. And since we ought to pray with you or for you, let God assist your weakness, He who brings the dead back to life.

Gregory was consecrated to the Church of Nyssa (Cappadocia Secunda) *in 372, by his brother the metropolitan, who aimed at increasing the number of his suffragans, in order to boost the authority of his own see—a normal practice in fourth-century Anatolia. He was arrested and sent into exile on a trumped up charge by order of the Arianizing Emperor Valens. He ministered for some time at Ibora (Iverönü), a small bishopric in the vicinity of Neo-Caesaraea, and was elected to the then vacant see of Sebastaea (Sivas) in Lesser Armenia. After the death of Valens (378), he caused his brother Peter, the youngest of the family, to be elected to the see of Sebastaea, and returned to Nyssa, at the latest in 380. The years following the death of Saint Basil (the 1st of January 379) saw Gregory successfully engaged in the negotiations preparatory to the Council of Constantinople (May-June 381). We know little about his later years. In 394, he was again present at a synod held in Constantinople. He died shortly thereafter, ca. 395.*

3

The Quest for Wisdom

If the date of 375 assigned by the early editors of Basil's letter 223 to Eustathios of Sebastaea is correct, we have there a sample of Basil's reminiscing over his own "conversion." Returning from Athens, he had visited hermits and Christian communities throughout the Middle East, settled in the solitude of the Iris, and dedicated his whole life to the edification of the Church, whatever the cost to his personal inclinations. Now he wrote to Eustathios, whose ascetic way of life had at first impressed him so much, but whose instability and stubbornness cruelly disappointed our Saint. More on the quarrel that opposed them to each other will be found below in chapter 7, "Priests and Hierarchs: Upholders of Orthodoxy."

BASIL TO EUSTATHIOS OF SEBASTAEA, LETTER 223 (375)

I have spent many a year in the pursuit of nothingness [τῇ ματαιότητι] and I have consumed almost all my youth in the vain attempt to acquire the teachings of a wisdom which is folly in God's eyes. And then, one day, as waking up from a deep slumber, I looked toward the wonderful light of the truth of the Gospel, and I saw the uselessness of the wisdom of the "rulers of this age, who are doomed to pass

away" [1 Co 2:6]. I wept abundantly on my miserable life
and prayed that a hand be extended to introduce me into
the principles of piety. Among other things I was eager to
straighten myself up, so spoiled I had been by my frequenta-
tion of frivolous people. Having read the Gospel and having
seen that the best starting point toward perfection was to get
rid of one's possessions and to share them with poor brethren,
to take no care for this life and to let our soul have no feeling whatever for the things here below, I wished to find one
of the brethren choosing this way of life, so that I could cross
with him over the stormy seas of life. I found many such
men at Alexandria, in other parts of Egypt, and in Palestine, in Coelesyria and Mesopotamia. I wondered at their
discipline of life, I wondered at their steadfastness in hardships, I was amazed at their constance in prayers, how they
prevailed over sleep, yielding to no bodily exigency, keeping
the affects of their soul always lofty and free from bondage,
in hunger and thirst, in cold and nakedness, never giving
attention to the body, never willing to worry about it. As
if they were living out of the flesh, they did show me by their
acts what it means to be a foreigner passing through this
world and to have our citizenship in heaven. I admired all
this, and I regarded the life of these men as blessed, for
they showed by their actions that they were "carrying in the
body the death of Jesus" [2 Co 4:10], and I wished that, as
much as was in me, I could emulate them. Since the secrets
of every one of us remain hidden, I imagined that a humble
apparel was a sufficient mark of humility and that a coarse
mantle, a belt, and sandals of raw leather were convincing
enough for me. Many tried to tear me loose from the society
of those ascetics, but I did not yield, seeing that they preferred
a life of renouncement to a life of laxity, and I envied them
for their unusual way of living. . . . The notion of God
which I had received since childhood from my blessed
mother [Emmelia] and from grandmother Macrina [the
elder] I have kept in me that it might grow; I did not exchange it for others, but I have completed the rudiment that
had been transmitted to me. A growing [plant], tiny at first,
becomes bigger but remains what it is without changing its

nature, developing itself as it grows; likewise, it seems to me that the doctrine itself did grow by degrees as life progresses. Let people, then, search their own conscience, consider the court of justice of Christ, and testify whether they have ever heard from us anything different of what we profess today.

BASIL TO EUSTATHIOS, PHILOSOPHER, LETTER 1 (357)

First, the addressee is not to be confused with Eustathios of Sebastaea in Lesser Armenia, whom we know from the preceding selection. He is a philosopher whom Basil tried vainly to trace throughout the Middle East in the course of his own peregrinations. That Eustathios is probably, like Basil and Gregory of Nazianzus, an "ex-Athenian."

. . . I have left Athens because of the renown of your philosophy, through disdain for the things from over there. I passed in a hurry through the city of the Hellespont [Constantinople], which I fled like no Ulysses ever fled the song of the Sirens. I admired Asia, but I was in a hurry to reach the metropolis [Caesaraea] for its beauty. After my arrival in the home country, I was looking forward to meeting you as a great advantage, but I did not find you. Thereupon I was hampered by reason of many unforeseen impediments. Either I managed to be sick and could not catch up with you, or I was incapable of joining you after you left. And finally, when I arrived in Syria, suffering a thousand miseries, I was prevented from joining my philosopher, who had gone to Egypt. So I had to leave once more and go myself to Egypt—a long and arduous journey, and still without reaching my goal. I felt so frustrated that I would have set out for Persia and run after you far away into the parts of the barbarians, for you went as far as that, so great was the malice of the devil. Or else I would have stayed here in the land of Alexander [Alexandria], and that is just what happened! I think that, had I not given up running after you like a fawn after a green twig, I might have gone to Nysa in India; if there had been a place at the extremity of the earth, you also would have been wandering there. But finally, now that you live in our region, if it was not given to me that we might come together for even a short while, that is because I was hindered by a long illness.

The quest for wisdom is not a matter of running after it from East to West, from Pontus to the Nubian sketes. Letter 2 of Saint Gregory of Nyssa discusses the arguments for and against the value of pilgrimages to the "Holy Land," very popular at the time. The letter is addressed to a certain "Kensitôr"; either a personal name, according to G. Pasquali, or is it the title of an officer holder: census taker, keeper of the taxpayers roll? Now the title may very well have become a local designation for the official in charge, the family name being virtually forgotten. Gregory, consulted by Kensitôr, expresses himself very bluntly. There is in those pilgrimages no inherent virtue of sanctification, unless the pilgrims are inspired by a vivid faith in the living Christ revealed in the Gospel. Saint Jerome, who incidentally was in friendly relationship to Gregory and to Gregory of Nazianzus, esteemed that pilgrimages to Jerusalem were at best unnecessary, and that most of the time they distracted the souls from the essentials of the faith.

GREGORY OF NYSSA, LETTER 2, TO KENSIOR, ON THOSE WHO GO TO JERUSALEM

You ask me, dear friend, to send you by letter an orderly account of what I think should be answered to all your questions. I feel that those who once applied themselves to a higher way of life shall profit by paying attention in all things to the words of the Gospel and, like those who rectify their purpose according to the rule, shall make straight what in their hands is crooked. Thus I believe that such a rule, straight and immutable—I mean, the discipline of the Gospel —will direct toward God those who apply themselves to it.

Therefore, since there are among those who have chosen for themselves a solitary and secluded life, some who make it a point of devotion to have seen the holy places in Jerusalem, where the marks of the sojourn of the Lord in the flesh are visible, it is advisable that we consider the ruling principle, whether these things guide us as by the hand to the observance of the commandments. If they are alien to the precepts of the Master, I fail to see what good can be accomplished, for lack of a prescriptive authority.

When the Lord called the blessed ones unto the inheritance of the kingdom of heaven, did he number among their obligations that they should set out toward Jerusalem? When he proclaimed the beatitudes [μακάρισμα], he included no such duty, which makes one neither blessed nor ready for the kingdom; let anyone who has some brain figure that out! For if it had any usefulness, should it not be deemed worthy to be sought for by the perfect? . . . Is it not the same discipline that is proposed both to men and women? Propriety is fitting for a life dedicated to the cultivation of wisdom [φιλοσοφία]. . . . But since, in the regions of the East, the hostelries, the wayside inns, and many cities, show licentiousness and indifference with regard to vice, how can it be that one passes through the smoke without his eyes being inflamed? When the ears are defiled, and the eyes defiled, the heart also receives unclean impressions through the ears and

the eyes. How is it possible to pass unaffected through those
infected places? Is it that people born in those parts, because
they are bodily living near the holy places of the Lord, forsake our regions and become richer? Or is it that the Holy
Spirit superabounds unto the people of Jerusalem, but passes
us over and is powerless with us? If the presence of the Lord
can be surmised from visible marks, shall we not think that
God would rather dwell in Cappadocia than in far-away
regions? For how numerous in our parts are the altars on
which the name of God is glorified! And there are countless
altars throughout the world! If grace were more abundant
in Jerusalem's holy places than elsewhere, then sin would
not haunt the inhabitants of the region as it does, for there
is no kind of vice to which they are not addicted: fornication,
adultery, theft, idolatry, witchcraft, jealousy, and murder;
such crimes are so common that nowhere else is there such
a readiness to kill in cold blood, moved by their greediness
and avidity, not unlike wild beasts wallowing in the blood
of some of their kind! And what happened in Jerusalem—
O irony!—should be regarded as proof that there is in those
places a more abundant grace?

But I know the objection of many against my arguments.
They say: "Why do you not make of all this a law for yourself? If it is useless in God's eyes to go to Jerusalem, why did
you leave on this vain journey?" So let them hear my defense:
my motive was the obligation of the life in which I have been
placed by Him who orders our lives, as I was commanded by
the Holy Synod [viz. the Council of Constantinople, 381]
to set out for the regions of Arabia in order to straighten
up the affairs of the Church in those parts. Since Arabia
borders on the region of Jerusalem, it was suggested that I
join the bishops of Palestinian Churches in view of the
troubled situation, for the sake of mediation. The most pious
emperor [Theodosius] granted us the use of the official means
of transportation, and we needed not undergo the incon-
veniences that plague other travelers. The chariot served for
us as a church and a monastery, for the psalmody in common
and the fasting unto the Lord during the entire journey. Let
no one be startled on our account, but accept our advice:

whatever met our eyes was for us a lesson. Even before we arrived, we had always confessed that Christ, when He appeared among men, is the true God, and our faith was neither diminished nor increased; we believed that He became man through the Virgin, even before we went to Bethlehem; that He arose from the dead, even before we went to the Sepulcher; as for His ascension to the heavens, we confessed it as true even before seeing the Mount of Olives. What we retained from our journey is that our faith gained by comparison something much more sacred than its external props. Therefore, you who fear the Lord, praise Him! A local change will not bring you closer to God, but no matter where you are, God will come to you, if only your soul is found a proper resting place where God can dwell and converse. . . . Therefore, dear friend, do exhort the brethren to move away from the things of the flesh unto the Lord; not from Cappadocia to Jerusalem.

The central theme of the Life of Moses *of Saint Gregory of Nyssa (texte critique, translated into French and commented by the late Cardinal Daniélou,* Sources Chrétiennes, *vol. 1 bis, Paris 1955), shall bring our third chapter to its conclusion: the quest for divine wisdom shall never end. The very transcendence of the object makes it that it will remain forever beyond our reach, since the* "Perfection of Virtue," *Gregory's subtitle of his book, consists essentially in the never-ending progress of the soul, for we are creatures of desire, and desire, as desire, vanishes as soon as it has reached its goal. Thus, perfection is itself an uninterrupted progression, and never attains to the fixity of a "state."*

GREGORY OF NYSSA, LIFE OF MOSES, II 225-226

Because there is nothing above to break the impetus of the soul, and because the very nature of the good is that it attracts those who look up toward it, the soul rises always, extending itself forward [συνεπεκτεινομένη] through the desire of heavenly things, as the Apostle says [Ph 3:13], and its flight will lead it always higher. Desirous as it is never to renounce to the summits which are above itself, and in view of what it has reached already, the soul is given a movement of never-ending ascension, and it finds always in its past achievements a new energy for soaring higher; for spiritual activity alone has the propriety of nuturing its strength while expending it, and not to lose, but rather to increase it through exercise.

We have here Platonism at its best. The number of places in which Gregory follows Plato almost word for word, especially in the Symposium, *is overwhelming. Will the movement of continuous progression toward the Fair, the Good, and Love—in se—not be interrupted brutally by death, or will the redeemed soul continue soaring from brightness to brightness? Judging from the theme of the* Life of Moses, *we do not see why death might put an end to the ascension of the soul, no longer weighted down by its earthly load of flesh and the burden of its sins. But rational speculations here are hopeless.* Altiora te ne quaesieris! *(Sirach 3:22).*

Here I would refer my readers to an essay I published in Diotima, Revue de recherche philosophique, *Athens 1983, pp. 30-39, under the title* "Vertu, épectase, perfection."

4

Monastic Ideal

Basil, writing to Gregory of Nazianzus from the solitude in Pontus (letters 2 and 22), sets forth the principles of spiritual life in a religious community. We have here a first sketch of what is known as "the Rules," which were to shape the life of his followers, and which left an indelible imprint on Benedictine life in the Latin West. The Christian living must aim at realizing the ideal of ἡσυχία (quietude) and at overcoming the dispersion of secular life; Basil's ἡσυχία corresponds in Western monasticism to the Benedictine "Pax," peace.

Christian charity should inspire the entire life of the brethren, a heavenly life, yet earthly as well; hence, Basil's insistence on the necessity of elementary kindness and of unaffected good manners, for which the brethren may have had some use, since a number of them seem to have been rather boorish, if we judge from Basil's remarks.

St Basil to Gregory of Nazianzus, Letter 2
(358-359?)

. . . One should aspire at keeping the mind in quietude [ἡσυχία]. The eye that wanders continually around, now sideways, now up and down, is unable to see distinctly what lies under it; it ought rather to apply itself firmly to the visible object if it aims at a clear vision. Likewise, the spirit of man, if it is dragged about by the world's thousand cares, has no way to attain a clear vision of the truth. . . . Each day arrives, each in its own way obscuring the mind; and the nights, taking over the cares of the day, deceive the soul with obnoxious phantasms. There is only one escape: withdraw from the world altogether. Now this withdrawal [ἀναχώρησις] does not mean that we should leave the world bodily, but rather break loose from the ties of "sympathy" of the soul with the body. This means to be without a city, without a house, without anything of our own, without property, without possessions, without resources, without affairs, without contracts, without being taught by men, but making ready to receive in our heart the imprint of divine teaching.

This litany of privative expressions, "without a city," "without a house," etc., is a favorite device of Basil, the rhetor turned hegumen. Renouncing the amenities of secular life is an ideal for monastics to live by, but will they ever realize it? The goal is elusive; it seems to remove itself farther and farther, even as one thinks one is going to attain it. May I be permitted to borrow the following lines from Nikos Kazantzakis who most likely did not quote from Basil? "Reach what you can; or rather, reach what you cannot! It is our duty to set ourselves an end higher than ourselves . . . to toil night and day to attain it. . . . No, not to attain it, but never to halt in the ascent" (Report to Greco).

Basil's frame of reference is a religious house in which everything is held in common at the discretion of the hegumen—shelter, possession, resources. The clause "without a partner of our choice," my rendering for Basil's ἀφιλέται-ρον, has become in Courtonne's French translation "sans amitiés particulières," the nightmare of spiritual directors and masters of novices in western religious houses! As a

*matter of fact, Basil never denies his attachment for Gregory
and occasionally declares his affection in hyperbolic terms:
"I breathe you more than I breathe air, and I live only when
I am with you" (Letter 6 to Gregory).*

The solitude [ἐρημία] offers a very great advantage for
our task. . . . Let therefore the site of the monastery be most
like our place here [Annisi], free from the commerce of men,
so that nothing may come from without and break the continuity of the "askesis," for a pious "askesis" nurtures the
soul with divine thoughts. Is there a greater happiness than
to imitate on earth the choir of angels? At daybreak, to get
up at once for prayer and honor the Creator with hymns and
canticles? Then, when the sun shines with its pure light, to
rush to work, to be accompanied everywhere with prayer
and, so to speak, to season our labor with the salt of hymns;
to establish the soul in joy and drive out sadness is the gift
and the comfort of the hymns. Quietude [ἡσυχία] is therefore the principle of purification of the soul, when the
tongue does not speak the words of men, when the eyes
do not turn all around to behold the complexion and the
proportion of bodies, when the hearing does not loosen the
spirit with sweet tunes composed for pleasure, or with jokes
or buffoon cries most apt to unnerve the strength of the
soul.

. . . The high road leading to the discovery of duty is the
study of the inspired Scriptures. In them are found rules of
action, and the lives of the blessed which the Scriptures have
transmitted to us are like living images of the godly life set
before us that we may imitate their good works.

. . . Prayers succeeding to lecture rejuvenate and invigor-
ate the soul, which is moved toward God by desire, for
beautiful is the prayer that impresses into the mind a clear
notion of God. This is properly the "inhabitation" [ἐνοί-
κησις] of God, to have God seated in oneself through memory. Thus we become a temple of God, when earthly cares

do not interrupt the continuity of memory, when the mind is not disturbed by unforeseen passions and when, fleeing from all things, the friend of God [ὁ φιλόθεος] withdraws unto God, drives out all incitements to evil, and holds fast to those practices that lead to virtue.

First of all, we must not be ignorant of the proper usage of speech, but rather ask questions peaceably and answer without seeking to be admired, not interrupting our interlocutor when he says something useful, nor desiring to throw in our own words with ostentation. We must trace a border line between talking and listening, learning without being ashamed, and teaching irreproachably. Only after having examined in ourselves that which we want to say shall we express it. We must be courteous in conversation, gentle in communicating with others; it is not through jokes that we must seek pleasantness, but through benevolent exhortations that we may gain sympathy.

After describing how one should converse with others, Basil passes without transition to what is proper for the brethren with regard to garment, food, and sleeping hours, as befits persons living in a religious community. The table of the monks shall be frugal. No mention is made of meat, an expensive luxury which anyway monks and common people could ill afford—not that meat as such was frowned upon as sinful. In his letter 14 to Gregory of Nazianzus, Basil mentioned the abundance of game and fish in the solitude of Pontus. Naukratios, his brother, who had retired in a nearby hermitage, used to go hunting and fishing, to add to the meager fare of the old people for whom he cared, and he met an accidental death, drowning in a whirlpool of the Iris.

[Letter 2, continued]

Let the tunic [χιτών] be maintained around the body by a belt, and this belt not high above the haunches—it would look effeminate; nor so loose that the tunic would flow—that is softness. Let not the gait be sluggish—the soul would be charged with laxity; nor impetuous and swaggering, which betrays rashness and aggressivity. The sole purpose of clothing is to provide a sufficient covering for the body, winter and summer. . . . To consider in a garment its nice color is no better than the prettifying which women seek by painting their cheeks and hair with borrowed cosmetics. . . . The footwear should be inexpensive, but appropriate to give good service.

In eating, one should not display the gluttony of a mad guzzler, but observe always restraint, moderation, and self-discipline regarding pleasures, without letting the mind idle away from the thought of God. . . . Prayers are offered before the meal, that we might be worthy of God's gifts, those which He grants us now and those He shall dispense later. Prayers after the meal are to give thanks for the present gifts and to ask for those which have been promised. Let an hour be assigned for the meal, recurring at the same time, so that out of the twenty-four hours of the day and night, only one be spent for the body; during the others, the ascete should be occupied with spiritual work. Sleep should be light, easy to shed, being measured to the needs of ascetic life. . . .

Here follows mention of what would become regular monastery services, ἀκολουθίαι, in the early morning the ὄρθρος, and toward the middle of the night the μεσο-νύκτιον.

[Letter 2, continued]

What the ὄρθρος is to other people must be the μεσο-
νύκτιον to ascetics. Indeed, the quiet of the night is most
beneficial to the soul when the ears and the eyes do not
convey to the heart noxious discourses or spectacles, when
the mind, recollected in itself alone, unites itself with God,
and when man corrects himself from sin by remembering
[God], sets unto himself limits to avoid evil, and seeks God's
help achieving that end toward which he exerts himself.

BASIL TO GREGORY OF NAZIANZUS, "ON THE PERFECTION OF MONASTIC LIFE," LETTER 22

---

*In 364, Basil, on the point of being ordained to the
priesthood by Eusebius, metropolitan of Caesaraea, had not
yet left the solitude of Pontus, where he would always return
with eagerness whenever the exigencies of the ministry as a
priest and a bishop made it possible. Letter 22 develops the
theme of letter 2. The familiar advice for community living
have now grown into a list of formal precepts, forty-eight in
number, following a short introduction in which Basil points
out that each one rests on the authority of Scripture. Each
paragraph begins with the formula* "Ὅτι δεῖ *or, in the
negative,* "Ὅτι οὐ δεῖ. *This catalogue of do's and don'ts
may have been prepared in collaboration with Gregory of
Nazianzus, who wrote to Basil in letter 6 (361): "We have
made these principles secure by means of written precepts
[*ὅροις γραπτοῖς] and canons [*κανόσιν]."*

1. The Christian ought to have thoughts worthy of his
heavenly calling and order his life to be worthy of the Gospel
of Christ.

2. The Christian must not let anything blow or drag him away from the remembrance of God, His will, and His judgments.

3. The Christian must not swear or lie, under pretence that in all things he is above the justice of the Law.

4. He must not blaspheme, curse, fight, avenge himself, render evil for evil, or act in anger.

5. One should be patient, whatever one has to suffer. Even though we have the right to rebuke the one who has wronged us, we must do this not in passion for having been wronged, but in the hope of correcting a brother, according to the precept of the Lord.

6. One must not say anything against an absent brother and slander him, even if what is said is true.

7. One should turn away from one who decries a brother.

8. One should not indulge in jesting.

9. One should not play the buffoon or suffer buffoons.

10. One should not speak idle talk, for it is neither useful to those who listen, nor necessary or permissible with regard to God. Those who work should apply themselves quietly to their task [μετὰ ἡσυχίαν] and leave speeches of exhortation to those entrusted with the judicious dispensation of the Word unto the edification of the faith, lest the Holy Spirit of God come to grief.

11. One is not permitted to accost brethren entering [the monastery] or to speak to them before those in charge of taking care of the general order would have examined whether this is agreeable to God for the common advantage.

12. One must not be a slave to wine or crave for meat, or generally delight in any food or drink, for the athlete ought to observe temperance in all things.

13. One must not hold as personal property something that is distributed to the brethren for their usage, nor store up anything; furthermore, if something is abandoned or thrown away, one must pick it up and regard it as the Master's property.

14. No one may be his own master, but mind and do all things as if one had been delivered by God in bondage to

the brethren, who are one's kin by the soul [ὁμοψύχοις]; each person at his own rank.

15. One must not grumble if necessary things are scarce, nor if toil is excessive, for it belongs to those in authority to decide these matters in each case.

16. One must not shout, or assume postures or a gait manifesting passion or wandering of the spirit away from the fullness of God's presence.

17. One ought to moderate one's voice as needed.

18. One must not reply to another, or treat him rashly or scornfully, but in all circumstances one ought to show fairness and respect unto all.

19. One must not wink cunningly with the eye and assume attitudes or gestures that may grieve a brother or manifest some contempt.

20. One must not take pride in garments or footwear; that is vanity.

21. One ought to use inexpensive things for the needs of the body.

22. One must not spend anything beyond what is necessary and to excess; that is abuse.

23. One must not aspire to honors, or claim the first places.

24. Everyone should esteem others more than himself.

25. One must not be rebellious.

26. He who does nothing while being able to work should not eat either. But he who is busy with a task to be performed exactly ought to apply himself with all the zeal of which he is able, unto the glory of Christ.

27. Everyone ought to do all things reasonably and with conviction, as approved by the leaders, even eating and drinking, to the glory of God.

28. One must not shift from one task to another without the agreement of those in charge of these sorts of things, unless being called suddenly, by evident necessity, to the help of one who lacks strength.

29. Everyone should stay at his own post and not overstep the limits of his assignment for reaching unto what had

not been commanded to him, unless those in charge judge that another needs help.

30. Nobody must be found wandering from workshop to workshop.

31. One should not do anything out of contentiousness.

32. One should not envy the reputation of another, or rejoice in his shortcomings.

33. One ought to deplore the faults of his brother for the love of Christ and feel sorry, but rejoice for what he did well.

34. One must not be indifferent toward sinners, nor unconcerned [about their sin].

35. If one has to reprove sinners, let it be with mercifulness, in the fear of God and in order to correct the sinner.

36. He who is reproved or blamed ought to take it with good will, realizing that it is for his own good.

37. One must not, if someone else is accused, contradict the accuser to his face or before others. If the accusation seems unreasonable, one should say a word in private to the accuser, and persuade him, or be persuaded by him.

38. Everyone as he is able should try to heal [with kindness] anyone who has something against him.

39. One must not bear a grudge against a man who has sinned and repents, but forgive him heartily.

40. He who says that he repents from sin should not only be contrite for the sin he has committed, but also make worthy fruits of repentance.

41. He who has been rebuked for first sins and was deemed worthy of pardon prepares for himself a judgment of anger worse than the previous [rebuke], if he sins again.

42. He who after a first and second warning persists in his fault ought to be reported to the hegumen, if this seems better than having him rebuked in public. If he does not amend himself, let him be removed from among the others like an object of scandal and "regarded as a heathen and a publican" [Mt 18:17] for the safety of those who cultivate obedience with zeal, according to the saying: "When the impious falls, the just are struck with fear"; but one should also mourn for him as for a limb severed from the body.

43. One should not let the sun set on an angry fit of a brother, lest night separate both from each other and leave an inexorable verdict in the day of judgment.

44. One should not wait for an occasion to amend oneself, because he cannot be certain of the morrow; many who have made many projects have not reached the morrow.

45. One should not let himself be fooled by a full belly, because it is a cause of nightmares.

46. One ought not be dragged into working immoderately beyond the limits of the sufficient; according to the words of the Apostle, "if we have food and covering, we should be satisfied" [1 Tm 6:8], for an abundance which exceeds the necessary displays greediness, and "greediness denotes idolatry" [Col 3:5].

47. One must not be avaricious [φιλάργυρον] or hoard unnecessary things.

48. He who comes to God should embrace poverty in all things and be transfixed [lit. *nailed,* καθηλωμένον] by the fear of God, according to him who said: "Nail thy flesh to the fear of me, for I have feared thy judgments" [Ps 118: 120, LXX].

May the Lord give you to receive our instructions with full assurance and bring forth worthy fruits of the Spirit to the glory of God, through God's grace and with the cooperation of our Lord Jesus Christ, Amen!

Observance of the rule is not enough if it is not animated by the charity that must inspire the whole life of a Christian. The precepts of Basil the monastic leader (ἡγούμενος; Russian "starets," pl. "startsy"). According to Dom Léon Lèbe, OSB, they were expanded, formally rewritten, and eventually clarified by Basil during the later years of his life, for the benefit of the monastic order as a whole. Thus edited, the monastic rules of Saint Basil were to inspire the spirituality and the regimen of the foundations of Saint Benedict, father of western monasticism (cf. Saint Basile, les règles monastiques, *éditions de Maredsous, 1969).*

The clerics of Neo-Caesaraea do not seem to have appreciated Basil's warning against a variety of sectarians who went along peddling "their follies with a stuttering tongue," under a deceptive appearance of piety. In part of letter 207, Basil attacks their untraditional practices and their display of unwarranted asceticism, extolling by contrast the common life of his monks and their liturgical service in conformity with the common usage of "all the Churches of God."

BASIL, TO THE CLERICS OF NEO-CAESARAEA, LETTER 207 (375)

. . . If you ask these troublemakers for the cause of their implacable and relentless assaults, it is that they read psalms and sing hymns on modes different from the usage that has prevailed among you, and similar reasons which had better be kept hidden. . . . In order to answer to their accusations about psalmody, with which our calumniators impress most simple-minded people, I shall say this: The practices that have obtained today in all the Churches of God are concordant and in mutual harmony. Here at home the people rise at night and go to the house of prayer. In grief and contrition they confess their sins to God with shedding tears. Then, standing up after the prayers, they begin the psalmody and, divided now into two choirs, they sing antiphonally; thus they strengthen their attention to the sentences from Scripture [τὰ μάτια], and make their unstable hearts more steady. Then one single reader is in charge of intoning the hymns, and the others respond. In this way, they pass the night, alternating psalmody with prayers. At dawn, all of them together, with one single heart and mouth, send up to the Lord the psalm of penitence [τῆς ἐξομολογήσεως ψαλμὸς, i.e. Ps 51, vulg. 50], and everyone makes David's words of repentance his very own. Now if this is your reason for turning away from us, you should turn away from the Egyptians as well, the Libyans of both Libyas, the Thebans, the Palestinians, the Arabs, the Phoenicians, the Syrians, and the people beyond the Euphrates; in short, all among whom vigils, prayers, and psalmody are held in honor. You object that these practices did not exist in the time of the great Gregory [the Wonderworker]; well, neither did those litanies for which you care so much! I do not say this to accuse you; I would like to see you living in tears and incessant repentance. As for ourselves, we do not do anything else but pray for the remission of our sins.

Orthodox Christians will easily recognize in Basil's sketch the basic structure of their Office of the Vigil (Great Vespers and Matins): the introductory prayers; the Psalter, divided into twelve stanzas (καθίσματα); the psalms ("I call upon Thee, hear me O Lord"); in the early dawn, the "Miserere" and the praises; at daybreak, the first hour.

That Basil's brethren and sisters in his monasteries were not all angels we know already from the foregoing. Now here is a downright ruffian, against whom Basil solicits the intervention of the provincial governor: a runaway "solitary" had sacked Basil's familial home at Neo-Caesaraea, after having assaulted the women who guarded the door. The fellow belonged with common jailbirds rather than in a monastic community.

BASIL TO CANDIDIANOS, PROVINCIAL GOVERNOR; LETTER 3, WRITTEN FROM ANNISI

A certain ruffian who lived with us at Annisi, without saying that some debt was still due to him, did not tell me anything after the death of the bursar. He did not claim for anything but what had been given to him; he did not threaten us that he would take his due by force if we gave him nothing, but then suddenly, with a few rascals of his sort, he attacked our town house, assaulted the women who guarded it, broke the doors, pillaged at random, grabbed his share of booty, and left the rest for any who wanted it. Lest we appear utterly defenseless in that extremity, as if we had been created to be assaulted, we beg you to show us the same zeal with which you have always rescued us in the past, since we had no other way to escape our predicament but by placing ourselves firmly under your authority. It would satisfy us if the mayor [πάγαρχος] had that fellow arrested and put in jail for a while. What prompts us is less our feeling of indignation at what we had to endure, than a need of security for the future.

5
Priests and Hierarchs: Their Calling

It is a common maxim that one does not, or ought not to, choose a priestly career as one chooses to become a lawyer, a pharmacist, or an architect. One is chosen. "No man takes this honor upon himself, but he that is called of God" (Heb 5:4). The words of instruction of the Apostle to Titus are equally valid: "If any man aspires to the office of a bishop, he desires a noble task" (1 Tm 3:1). The life of the Three Hierarchs is a running commentary on those seemingly contradictory principles, diversely illustrated in the correspondence of Basil and the two Gregorys.

The very circumstances of the life of Basil, not his own choice, demanded that the hegumen of the community on the Iris be able to dispense the divine mysteries to the solitaries. The letter in which he announced his ordination to his friend Gregory has not been preserved, but we possess Gregory's answer to it, letter 8. Basil had not sought the charge of the priesthood, and Gregory of Nazianzus showed a similar reluctance against being ordained, perhaps even more pronounced.

GREGORY OF NAZIANZUS TO BASIL, LETTER 8
(ca. 364)

I praise the preamble of your letter. What is there in you which should not be praised? You too, like us, have been enrolled by constraint, when we have been forcibly promoted to the priesthood. Certainly it was not something that we were striving for! We can sincerely attest one to the other, more than anyone else, that we were well satisfied with a pedestrian philosophy: remaining here below. It may have been better that this did not happen, but I do not know what to say, as long as I am in ignorance of the designs of the Spirit. Since this is the way things happened, we must accept them, it seems to me, especially on account of the time which loosens many heretic tongues against us; so we must not neglect the demands of our own life, or disappoint the hope of those who believe in us.

Basil certainly did not choose for himself the direction of the Cappadocian churches, especially in an era of trouble, but he was prevailed upon by his brethren in the priesthood and the episcopate to accept the charge and to be consecrated to the see of Caesaraea. The letters he received from the friends who had "campaigned" for him, and his own reactions, make it plain. Here are a few samples. We begin with a letter from Gregory the elder, the father of Gregory of Nazianzus. It is addressed to Eusebius of Samosata. Prior to the editions of the Benedictines of Saint Maur, it had been mistakenly attributed to Basil.

GREGORY THE ELDER, BISHOP OF NAZIANZUS, TO
EUSEBIUS, BISHOP OF SAMOSATA (SYRIA),
WRITTEN BEFORE 370. (Text in Basil's correspondence
[Budé], letter 47)

"Who shall give me wings like those of a dove?" [Ps 55:6] or how should my old age be renewed, so that I could go over to Your Piety, relieve the craving I have to be with you, tell you all my sorrows, and find from you some comfort in my afflictions? After the death of the blessed Bishop Eusebius [of Caesaraea], it was not a mean apprehension that took hold of us! Would not those who spied upon the Church of our metropolis and strove at filling it with the weeds of heresy seize now the occasion to uproot through their evil teachings the piety which had been sown so laboriously in the souls of men and to tear the unity of the Church as they have done in many other Churches? When letters of the clergy were sent to us, I looked all around and I remembered your charity, your right faith, and the zeal you always had for the Churches of God. For these reasons I sent the beloved Eustathius, our concelebrant [συνδιάκονος], to pray instantly Your Dignity that, above all your past labors for the Churches, you would still comfort my old age by adding this task for the present: straighten up the renowned piety of the right Church [τῇ ὀρθῇ Ἐκκλησίᾳ] by giving it, together with us, if we are to take part with you in this excellent work, a shepherd after the Lord's will, capable to steer His people. We have in front of us a man whom you know very well. If we are deemed worthy to obtain him, I know that we shall gain a great assurance with God, and procure an immense advantage to the people entrusted to us. But I pray you again, and I shall pray you many times, that you put all wavering aside and come to meet with us before the hardships of the winter season.

The "campaign" was not as peaceful as Gregory of Nazianzus, acting as chancellor of his father the bishop, would have wished. While recommending the candidacy of Basil in the strongest terms, he shows himself unexpectedly touchy, and complains of time-wasting bickerings between the bishops of the province and of their lack of appreciation for his advice and his person.

GREGORY OF NAZIANZUS TO THE BISHOPS OF
CAPPADOCIA, LETTER 43 (June to September 370)

How lovable you are, O lovers of men, charitable beyond measure! You have invited us to come to the metropolis; I suppose, to deliberate about a bishop; at least this is what I understand, but you do not make it clear whether it is necessary for us to go, nor what for, nor when; you just inform us suddenly that you are on your way. It looks as if you did not want to show us the slightest respect, did not desire our collaboration, but were eager to dissuade us and ward off our opposition. If that is what you planned, we will bear the insult, but we will let you know our feeling just as it is. Of course some will cast their vote for one candidate, some for another, as it happens always in such cases, according to their character or their interest. But we cannot prefer anyone to our most honored friend the priest Basil. Where, among those we know, could we find a man more eminent by his life, more powerful by his words, or so completely adorned with an outstanding virtue? If you object to his poor health, it is not an athlete you have to elect, but a teacher; remember also that all is possible to Him who strengthens the weak, if there are any, and who looks after them. If you agree, we shall be present and assist you, both spiritually and bodily. But if the way ahead is already preset, or if the factions prevail over the right, we will be happy to have been bypassed. Now this is your own affair, and pray for me!

Letter 40 of Gregory of Nazianzus to Basil, and the letter 41, addressed to the Christians of Caesaraea by Gregory the elder, bishop of Nazianzus, refer to the condition of the provincial capital of Cappadocia, disturbed by the anti-Nicene faction, when Archbishop Eusebius died in June 370. At that time, both Basil and his friend Gregory were in the order of priesthood, the latter as helper to his father the bishop of Nazianzus, and Basil in the service of Eusebius. Obviously Basil was well placed to judge the situation in Caesaraea, but little inclined to react positively, which caused Gregory to upbraid him for his inertness. In fact, Gregory and his father the bishop of Nazianzus considered Basil eminently qualified to become the successor of Eusebius, and the letter to the Christians of Caesaraea nominates Basil as a most desirable candidate. After some delay, the election of Basil to the metropolitan see of Caesaraea took place toward the end of the ecclesiastical year (autumn 370).

GREGORY OF NAZIANZUS TO BASIL, LETTER 40
(ca. June 370)

Be not amazed if I seem to say something unexpected, which nobody has said yet. You have, so it seems to me, the reputation of being steadfast, stable, and of a solid mind, but several of your counsels are more naïve than prudent. He who is free from malice is not soon inclined to suspect malice in others, and this is almost what is happening. You called us to the metropolis to hold counsel on the choice of a bishop; a nice pretext, quite convincing! You feigned to be sick, about to breathe your last, eager to see us and speak faltering words of farewell; I do not know what for, nor how our presence might help the affairs. . . . When I saw bishops rushing to the city, I wondered at first why you did not see what is advisable and why you did not ward off the evil gossips of people eager to calumniate the most irreproachable. Secondly I wondered why you did not realize that you and I, who have the same mind and life and everything in common, had to share the same predicaments, for God has harmonized us from the beginning. Thirdly—if I may also say this—do you not think that it is the most pious men who ought to be promoted, and not the most powerful and the most "popular"? . . . If this seems good to you, make up your mind, and keep away from those who are in the midst of the turmoil, a sorry plight! . . . I shall visit Your Piety when the trouble has abated and when the time is right, to do whatever is advisable, and then I will upbraid you some more, and more severely.

LETTER 41, ADDRESSED TO THE CHURCH AT CAESARAEA
By GREGORY THE ELDER, BISHOP OF NAZIANZUS
(Late Summer 370)

I am a poor pastor, head of a little flock and the smallest of the ministers of the Spirit, but grace is not limited by narrow borders. Let therefore even the little ones be free to speak, especially when important matters of public interest are discussed, and when the advisers are older people, who happen to have more wisdom than the crowd. You are not deliberating about worthless trivia, but about such matters as will affect the community for better or for worse, according to whether or not they are treated right. For your problem is about the Church for whom Christ has suffered, and about who shall call her and lead her to God. The eye, as we have heard [Mt 6:22], is the lamp of the body; not only the eye that sees and is seen bodily, but the eye, the organ and object of spiritual vision. Now the bishop is the lamp of the Church; this is evident to you, even if we do not write it. . . . The entire Church is to be cared for, being the body of Christ; and especially our Church, who has been since the origin and now is the mother of nearly all Churches; so is she now accounted. The eyes of all look toward her like the circle toward its center, not only because of the right doctrine she has preached from the beginning, but because of the grace of concord with which she was manifestly endowed by God. . . . I am sure that there are among you others who are worthy of presiding in such an important city, guided for a long time by outstanding leaders; however, among those of you who are worthy, I cannot prefer any to our own son the priest Basil, most beloved of God; God is witness of what I say! Basil is a man whose life and mind are pure, alone among all others, or indeed above them; he would be able to stand in the midst of the present trouble and the wild talk of the heretics. I write this to the priests, to the monks, to those in authority, to those sitting in the assembly, and to all the people. If you agree with this and if your votes prevail, rightly and wisely, since they are cast according to God, I am and I shall be present spiritually; or rather, I have already set my hand to the work, and I trust in the Spirit. If you decide otherwise and not this way, or if the affair was decided according to factions and kinship, if the accuracy of the vote was still disturbed at the hand of the mob, do what seems good to you; we shall keep in readiness here.

Gregory congratulates Basil on his elevation to the see of Caesaraea, which took place in September 370 (the beginning of the civil and the ecclesiastical year). He will not join his friend and will continue assisting his aged father as a priest in the episcopal curia at Nazianzus. He fears that the elevation of Basil to the metropolitan see might render difficult their mutual friendship, which had always expressed itself with utter frankness.

GREGORY OF NAZIANZUS TO BASIL, LETTER 45
(After September 370)

When I learned that you had been elevated to this lofty throne, and that the victorious Spirit had placed on a stand the lamp which had never ceased to shine bright, I must say: I rejoice! How could I do otherwise, seeing that the Church as a whole is in a sore state and in need of being firmly taken in hand. However, I did not rush toward you nor will I, and you should not ask me to hasten to come. First, it is in order to safeguard your dignity, for you should not seem to recruit partisans tastelessly and rashly, as your enemies would allege. Secondly, I have to steady myself and avoid provoking jealousy. Maybe you will say: "When shall you come, and how long will you delay your coming?" Till God commands me to, and until the shadows of those who attack us and decry us have passed by. For the lepers, I am sure, shall not forever hold up David from entering into Jerusalem [cf. 2 Sm 5:6].

We have observed repeatedly the shifting moods of Saint Gregory of Nazianzus, alternating from moments of deep repression to unbounded enthusiasm. They denote an instability due in part to his poor health—contrasting with Basil's composure—at a time when both of them were subject to trying circumstances. This feature may explain Gregory's tentative ideas to withdraw through flight. When prevented from taking possession of his see of Sasima, he attempted to seek refuge "in the desert"; after the death of his parents, he retired surreptitiously to Seleucia of Isauria where he learned of Basil's death in 379; after a riot during the Paschal solemnities in Constantinople, he resigned his charge; back in Cappadocia, he found himself exposed to the bickerings of local bishops; and his final retreat in the country estate of Kerbela did not bring him peace, as he complained of harassment by undesirable neighbors.

Letter 80 Philagrios, a friend of Gregory, was written in a moment of depression, perhaps from Constantinople, or after his return to Cappadocia. The addressee has been erroneously identified as a rhetor named Eudoxios, following an error of the early editions of Gregory of Nazianzus' letters (see Gallay, tome I, p. 103, note 1).

GREGORY OF NAZIANZUS TO PHILAGRIOS, LETTER 80
(After 379)

You ask about our situation; very bad! I do not have Basil any more, nor Kaisarios, my brother in the Spirit and by blood. "My father and my mother have forsaken me," shall I cry with David [Ps 27:10]. My body is sore; old age is on my head! Entanglement of worries, business harassments! Friends not to be trusted, the Church without a pastor! The good is lost, evil laid bare! Sailing in the dark, light nowhere! Christ asleep [Mt 8:24]. What has one not to bear? There is only one end to my troubles: death. And the future scares me, judging from what has happened thus far.

Letter 130, to Prokopios, a government official in Constantinople, contrasts sharply with the billet to Philagrios. Gregory is now in a high mood. He had always held the Council of Nicaea in high regard, because it had defined an essential dogma of the Church Universal, the "consubstantiality" of the Son with the Father (ὁμοούσιος), but he had little use for a multiplicity of local synods, liable to deteriorate into small parleys and doing not much good. Gregory, in retirement after the First Council of Constantinople (381), excuses himself to Prokopios, who had invited him to a synod of bishops, held in the capital in the summer of 382.

GREGORY OF NAZIANZUS TO PROKOPIOS, LETTER 130
(ca. 382)

Here is what I feel like writing: to tell you the truth, above all flee the reunions of bishops! I have never seen any having a good result and solving bad problems—if they do not aggravate them! Always quibbles and discussions having neither rhyme nor reason, and please do not take me for a rambunctious fellow when I write this to you! One would be charged sooner with perversity for correcting the others than effectively uprighting them! That is why I wrap myself in my thoughts, judging that the only security of the soul is quietude [ἡσυχία]. Now my ill health helps me to maintain my decision. I am almost on the point of breathing my last, and unable to do anything by myself. For this reason, let Your Magnanimity excuse us, and persuade our most pious Basileus [Theodosius] not to reproach us with indifference, but rather to forgive our infirmity. He knows how he permitted us to retire [from our charge], when we begged for this only favor.

*"Woe is me!" is Gregory's mood just before this retire-
ment, illustrated by letter 182. Writing to Gregory of Nyssa
on his return from Constantinople and readying himself to go
into retirement by leave from Emperor Theodosius, he is
eager to make his canonical status clear: he had been regularly nominated and consecrated to the see of Sasima, but had
found it occupied by Anthimos. He had never been called
or consecrated to the see of Nazianzus, but had merely accepted to help his aging father, the bishop, after whose death
he remained as provisional caretaker, the see of Nazianzus
being kept vacant.*

GREGORY OF NAZIANZUS TO GREGORY OF NYSSA,
LETTER 182 (383)

Woe is me, that my sojourn here has been extended!
The worst is that we are caught in a conflict of factions and
we have not maintained the peace that we had received from
the holy fathers. This peace—I know that you will resurrect
it by the power of the Spirit which sustains you and your
actions. As for us, I am only asking that no one would tell
lies about us or about the lord-bishops; it is not against us
that they have called another hierarch; they have not rejected
us nor are they hostile to us. But, having addressed to them
many prayers on account of my health—cadaverous!—and
fearing meanwhile that the Church would not be cared for,
I asked them this favor which is not against the canons and
would let me catch my breath: Let a pastor be given to the
Church! Such a one was given to them thanks to your
prayers, and worthy of Your Piety; I place him into
your hands. I mean the respected Eulalios, the bishop most
beloved of God, in whose hands may I give up my last
breath! If anyone thinks that one should not consecrate in
the lifetime of the hierarch in charge, let him rather know

that this should not make him prevail against us, for it is manifest to all that we have not been promoted to the see of Nazianzus, but of Sasima, although only for a while, for the sake of my father, regarding those who had petitioned us that we would accept the direction of the Church at Nazianzus as a foreigner.

A certain "Gigantios" had invited Gregory to visit him in his retreat in Cappadocia. An epigram of Gregory suggests that he is playing on the name of his correspondent, in reality Signatios (see the note in Gallay, tome 1, note additionelle, p. 131). Gregory had to decline the invitation on account of his poor health; the letter is a paean for the restoration of Orthodoxy.

GREGORY OF NAZIANZUS TO GIGANTIOS, LETTER 100
(Latter Part of 381)

Delighted by your invitation, I am still more delighted by what you write, not because of the compliments—that is unimportant—but because you think correctly and because the ties of charity that bind you to us are the hope of the same rewards and the sincere adoration of the Trinity, the Trinity whose name we utter more frequently than we breathe, whether or not there is danger in so doing. For the rest, we leave it to the circumstances, but our faith we keep immutably in our souls as the only riches inaccessible to envy and truly our own. And I myself, when I think of all those things, the tribulations that assailed us and assail us still, of capricious annoyances from above and from below, of the war which some war-loving people wage upon us who have not wronged them; when I only look on the sole fact that I have been judged worthy of becoming a herald of truth, whereas the sound doctrine was rejected and exiled contemptuously "in a dry and weary land where no water is" [Ps 63:1], it is too little for me to say that I throw back every anguish, but I am overjoyed to have been esteemed worthy of favors greater than me. Why do I write that? It is because I want to show that there is no solid friendship and intimacy except with those who have the same feelings. And those who have the same feelings—what sensible man would intentionally forsake them? Is there a greater feast than a feast passed in their company? If illness and winter shackle my good will, I shall bear the pain myself; but forgive us, and wish for another occasion of coming together.

The character, or lack of character, of Gregory of Nazianzus—the word is probably too strong—threatened once more to wreck his friendship with Basil, who had charged him with inaction, for his refusal to take a position in the conflicts of jurisdiction which opposed the bishops of Cappadocia to one another, following the division of the province by Emperor Valens. Gregory's letters 48 and 49 are his answers to Basil's criticisms.

GREGORY OF NAZIANZUS TO BASIL, LETTER 48
(ca. Easter 372)

We are tired of being blamed on your account and of apologizing unto those who know our past and understand the present situation. What is more ridiculous and deplorable is to find ourself both victim and accused; that is just what happens now. Some accuse us of this, the others of that, each one according to his temper or according to the measure of his anger toward us. The most friendly ones accuse us of disdain and say we are rejected after having been used like a vulgar, worthless utensil, or like those stays for building a vault, which one removes as useless once the construction is ended. Let us pay no attention to such people, and let them say what they please; nobody should restrain their freedom of speech. . . . Now I will show you how I feel, but do not get mad at me. I will tell you what I cried aloud, overwhelmed by emotion. I did not boil with anger, I was not so upset that I would lose my reason, unaware of what I was saying. I will not take arms, I will not learn to fight any more than I did when the situation invited a fight, when everyone was armed and in a fury. I will not fight against the bellicose Anthimos, even though he is a fighter out of season, for I am defenseless, unfit for war and laid open to wounds. Go fight him if you wish—necessity often makes weaklings warlike!—or else recruit fighters to guard the passes when he comes for "stealing your mules" ["he," the usurper of the see of Sasima, to which Gregory had been elected], like Amalek blocking the road to Israel [Ex 17:8 ssq]. Instead of all that, give us peace! Why should I fight for piglets and poultry which do not even belong to me, as if they were souls or canonical rules? Why deprive the metropolis of her "splendid Sasima," or unveil and reveal your secret thought, which had better remain hidden? Be a man, be strong, and draw all things to your own credit, like the rivers draw the brooks toward them. Do not give preference to our friendship and to an intimacy that proceeds from virtue and piety, and do not worry to know whether your actions shall be judged rightly. Belong only to the Spirit! As for me, I shall draw from your friendship this one benefit: not to put my trust in friends, and prefer nothing to God!

GREGORY OF NAZIANZUS TO BASIL, LETTER 49
(ca. Easter 372)

You reproach me with inaction and laziness because I have not taken possession of that Sasima of yours, because I do not act like a bishop should, and because I do not rush into the fray like a dog on a piece of meat. For me the greatest action is inaction and—that you may know my strong side —I am so proud of being inactive that on this point I am a model of magnanimity to all. If they would imitate me, all of them, there would not be any contention between the Churches, and faith would not be torn to pieces, by being taken as a weapon in personal disputes!

We close this chapter with a letter of Saint Basil written to Amphilochios, a young lawyer, cousin of Gregory of Nazianzus, who had heard and heeded the call to the priesthood. In 374, he was elected to the see of Iconium in Pisidia, made famous by the predication of Saint Paul. Here is Basil's "charge" to the new bishop.

SAINT BASIL TO AMPHILOCHIOS, ELECTED BISHOP OF ICONIUM IN PISIDIA, LETTER 161 (374)

Blessed is God, who from every generation chooses those who please Him, who distinguishes the choice vessels and uses them for the service of the holy things [πρὸς τὴν λειτουργίαν τῶν ἁγίων]. It is He who—as you say yourself that you fled, not from us, but from the call which you expected to receive through us—it is He who caught you in the inescapable net of His grace and led you to the heart of Pisidia, in order that you catch men unto the Lord, and drag from the abyss to light those whom the devil had caught.

Act like a man and be strong; march in front of the people the right hand of the Most High entrusted to you. Steer your ship prudently, stand above the tempests raised by heretical winds, keep your vessel from sinking in the briny and bitter waves of perverse doctrine, and wait for the still-ness which the Lord shall give when a voice is found worthy to wake Him up, that He rebuke the winds and the sea [Mt 8:26 and paral.].

If you wish to visit us who are driven by a long illness toward the inescapable issue, do not tarry or wait for us to give you a sign, for you know that to the heart of a father every occasion is welcome for embracing a dear son, and that the disposition of the soul is better than any discourse. Do not complain that the burden is above your strength. Supposing that you were alone to bear the load, it still would not be too heavy but quite bearable if the Lord carries it together with you, for, says the Psalmist, "cast your burden unto the Lord, and He will make good for it" [54:23]. Only let us exhort you to be watchful in all things, lest you yield to damnable practices; rather, amend previous abuses through the prudence that God gave you; for Christ has sent you, not to follow others, but to be yourself the leader of those who are to be saved. And we pray you to intercede for us, so that if we are still in this life, we may be found worthy to see you in your Church; but should we die first, we shall meet with you in the Lord.

6
Priests and Hierarchs:
Shepherds of the Sheep

The Three Hierarchs had to administer their Churches in the most trying circumstances. Orthodoxy was a minority in the midst of a medley of heterodox and heretics, who were often favored by local officials. On the political side, the Church aimed at establishing a modus vivendi *with the civil power, which was generally inclined to lean upon the majority. Whether they liked it or not, the bishops had to acknowledge the pluralism of the society and realized that true faith was not something they could ram down the throat of reluctant people.*

The Cappadocian hierarchy had to face some important changes in the government of the province: In 371, Emperor Valens reorganized the administration of the province by dividing it into two eparchies: Cappadocia Prima, *the eastern part of the province with the capital Caesaraea (Kayseri); and* Cappadocia Secunda, *the southwestern part, with the capital Tyana, itself an insignificant little town, but strategically located on the road to Archelaïs (Aksaray), Ancyra (Ankara), Nicaea (Iznik), and Constantinople. There were precedents: Diocletian, emperor from 284 to 305, had divided Armenia into Greater and Lesser Armenia, the latter being contiguous with the eastern parts of Pontus. Basil, consecrated archbishop of Caesaraea in 370, had as his opposite number in the imperial service the "archôn" of the eparchy, with whom he maintained correct relations. The towns of Nyssa and Nazianzus were now under the jurisdic-*

tion of the eparch of the Cappadocia Secunda, *and it was unavoidable that the influence of the bishop of Tyana would increase, for better or for worse.*

In view of the situation created by the imperial decrees, Basil explained to Amphilochios, the bishop of Iconium in Pisidia, his ideas on the reorganization of the churches of Isauria, a mountainous region on the northern slopes of the Taurus, east of Pisidia. Churches had grown at random, without much regard for canonical order, and they were often at odds with one another. Basil advocated a central authority for the sake of a more efficient service to local communities. This was an ideal; if it could not be realized, at least Amphilochios might supervise a modicum of reorganization.

BASIL TO AMPHILOCHIOS, BISHOP OF ICONIUM, LETTER 190 (374)

You have shown anxiety concerning the problems of the churches in Isauria in a manner worthy of your modesty and your zeal. That it would be more profitable to the greater number if the charge were divided among many bishops is evident, I think, to anyone, and this did not escape your attention, for you have described the situation nicely and made it known to us. But it is not easy to find men who are worthy. . . . As you know yourself, most of the time men under authority conform their *mores* to those of their superiors. Perhaps it would be better that one well-tested man, one alone—if it is easy to find such a one—be made to preside over the city and be entrusted, at his own risk, with the administration of all things in detail. Only let him be a true servant of God, a worker of whom one would not be ashamed, not seeking his own advantage, but the advantage of many, that they be saved [1 Co 10:33]. If he judges himself not to be up to prospective worries, he should secure co-workers for the harvest [Mt 9:37]. And if we find such a man, I believe that, though he be alone, he shall be worth many and be more useful to the churches inasmuch as he will take better care of the souls. While this is not easy to realize, we should begin by procuring diligently competent leaders for those small towns and boroughs that are episcopal sees for a longer time, and then we shall re-establish the bishop of the provincial capital. But one may fear that perhaps the one we propose might become an obstacle to our project, and that we would soon be fighting with our own people, should he aim at heading the majority and refuse to recognize the ordinations of the bishops. This is a heavy charge, and if time does not permit, then apply yourself to the following: have the territory that belongs properly to the bishop of Isauria duly surveyed, because he assigns at random suffragan bishops from neighboring districts. Whatever would remain to be done, leave it to us. When the time is favorable, we will appoint as bishops men whom we esteem best qualified, after a rigorous investigation.

We read in chapter 2 a fragment of a letter to the Neo-Caesaraeans (letter 204), in which Basil hoped to make of his Pontic ancestors a recommendation for himself; the city was at that time (375) in a state of general unrest, owing to the jealousy of the bishop, Atarbios, a relative who believed himself to be the one-man champion of Orthodoxy. He had accused Basil of laxity in dealing with some heretics who appeared ready to recant their errors. A stern hegumen in the community of the Iris, and a firm ruler of his archdiocese in the heart of Anatolia, Basil was nonetheless ready to accept at face value the assurance that recent converts gave of their sincerity, unless the deceit was manifest.

BASIL TO THE PEOPLE OF NEO-CAESARAEA, THROUGH THEIR PRIESTS. LETTER 204 (375)

. . . Deceitful calumnies have filled your ears; our life and our faith in God have been the object of calumny. I know that a calumniator inflicts damage to three persons at a time: the one he is decrying, the one whom he addresses, and himself. I would have kept silent on the prejudice caused to us; know this well. It is not that I disregard the esteem you show me—how could I?—lest I would seem to forfeit it, I am writing this letter to plead my cause now. But I see that, of the three persons who have been hit, it is I who have suffered the least. For if I am deprived of you, truth itself is stolen from you. . . . To this hour, by the grace of the One who has called us through a holy entreaty to the full knowledge of Him, we are conscious not to have admitted into our heart any thought adverse to sound doctrine, and our soul was never defiled by the odious blasphemy of the Arians. If we have at times welcomed some of their disciples who longed for our communion, who kept their distress hidden in their heart, whose words were pious words, or who did not contradict what we were saying, we would not reverse today our judgment on them, but rather follow the decisions prejudged by the vote of our fathers. I have received from our blessed father Athanasius, bishop of Alexandria, a letter which I have in my hands and which I show to those who wish. He orders clearly that if someone recants the heresy of the Arians by professing the Nicene faith, he should be accepted without hesitation. Athanasius quoted for me the unanimity of the bishops of Macedon and Achaïa on this policy. Thinking that it was necessary to follow so great a man because of the authority of the legislators, and since I hoped to receive the reward promised to the peacemakers, I have admitted into our communion those who made profession of the Nicene faith. . . . It would be more correct to judge us, not according to one or two who do not walk in the path of truth, but according to the multitude of the bishops who throughout the *oikoumenè* are united with us by the grace of the Lord. Ask those of Pisidia, of Lycaonia, of Isauria, of the two Phrygias, all those from Armenia your neighbors, the Macedonians, the Achaians, the Illyrians, the Gauls, the Spaniards, all the Italians, Sicilians, Africans, those who form the sound part of Egypt or who remain from among the Syrians, they all send us letters and receive our replies. Through their letters addressed to us you will understand, and through the letters which we send them in response you will realize that we are all of the same mind and of the same opinion. The one, therefore, who turns away from our fellowship—have no illusion on this—has cut himself from the Church as a whole.

Upholding the unity of the Churches professing the faith of Nicaea had been the constant preoccupation of the Three Hierarchs. They had worked together toward convening the Council of 381 in Constantinople. Basil was obsessed with the necessity of maintaining and developing contacts with the Churches in the West. In a sense, it proved too late: the two halves of Christendom, separated from each other by culture, language, institutional setup, and liturgical customs, were drifting apart, inexorably. The exchange of the kiss of peace and the lifting of excommunications by the Pope and the Ecumenical Patriarch in our days are certainly hopeful signs, but the object of hope is "a distant good and not easily obtainable"!

The title given by the manuscripts and the early editions to Basil's letter 70 is misleading: letter 70 is not an epigraph, but a pathetic appeal to Damasus, pope of Rome from 366 to 384. The old editions of the letters give for this one the date of 371, but this seems too early: ten years before the Council of Constantinople (381)!

BASIL, "ON A SYNOD," LETTER 70

To renew the laws of antique charity and the peace of the fathers, this heavenly and salutary gift of Christ which alas has withered away, to bring it back to the point of its origin appears to us necessary and fruitful. I know that it will be agreeable to your Christ-loving heart, for what can be more pleasing than to see people who are separated by vast stretches of land being united through charity into a single harmony of the members in the body of Christ? Nearly all the Orient, most honored Father, that is the Orient from Illyria to Egypt, is shaken by a violent tempest because the old heresy sown by Arius, the enemy of truth, reappears unashamedly today and, like a bitter root, bears deadly fruits. It may prevail in the future because those in charge of the right doctrine in every locality have been expelled from the Churches by calumnies and insults, and because those who imprison the souls of simple people hold the power. We had expected as the unique deliverance from these evils that in your compassion you would visit us; your outstanding charity has always guided us in the past, and the more cheerful prospect of your visit had comforted us for some time. But seeing our hope deceived, we cannot refrain ourselves, and we come to beg you by this letter to stand up to help us and send some envoys who partake of our feelings, either to reconcile the dissidents and restore friendship among the Churches of God, or at least to make the authors of the disturbance better known to you, so that you may judge clearly from now on those with whom it is proper to have communion. After all, we are not asking for anything new, but only for what was common to all our blessed elders and friends of God, especially among you. For we know that according to tradition, having interrogated our fathers and being instructed by the letters still kept by us, we know that Dionysios, that most blessed bishop, [Dionysios of Turio in *Magna Graecia,* bishop of Rome from 261 to 272] distinguished in your region for the orthodoxy of his faith and his other virtues, used to address letters to our Church at Caesaraea, comforted our fathers by these letters, and sent envoys to redeem our imprisoned brethren. Now our affairs are more critical and more sinister, and demand a greater attention. For it is not the ruin of earthly houses but the usurpation of Churches we deplore, not the enslaving of bodies but the enslaving of souls, every day, by the champions of heresy. Therefore if you do not arise now to succor us, soon you shall find no one to whom you could extend your hand, because all will have fallen under the power of heresy.

BASIL TO THE MOST HOLY BRETHREN, THE BISHOPS IN THE OCCIDENT. LETTER 90 (372)

The good God, who always joins consolation with tribulations, gave us even now, in the abundance of pains, to find a measure of comfort in the letters which our most reverend father bishop [Athanasius of Alexandria] has received from your uprightness and which he has forwarded to us. It shows forth a wholesome faith and gives proof of an unopposed union and concord, as it reveals also shepherds who follow in the footsteps of the Fathers and feed wisely the people of the Lord. It all gave us much joy and put an end to our distress; it brought about, so to speak, a brief smile to our soul, after the gloomy turmoil which actually afflicted us. The Lord has still increased His consolation by sending our dear son and fellow-minister [συνδιάκονος] Sabinos, who has fed our souls by his accurate description of the good that is being done in your country and, having learned by experience our situation, will make it clearly known to you. So, to begin with, you shall fight with us through zealous and diligent prayer to the Lord, and furthermore you will not refuse to bring to exhausted Churches the encouragement that is in you; for the Church suffers here, most reverend brethren, and gives way under the continuous assaults of its enemies, as a ship in the midst of the sea is tossed about by the waves beating repeatedly, if she were not soon visited by the goodness of the Lord. Just as we regard your mutual concord and unity as our own good, so do we entreat you to sympathize with our dissensions and, because of the distance between our countries, not to separate yourselves from us, but to receive us into the harmony of one single body, since we are made one in the community of the Spirit. [Here Basil describes the Arian persecution of the Orthodox in the eastern Churches.] . . . If there is a consolation of charity, a communion in the Spirit, if you have bowels of compassion, make haste to succor us. Take on the zeal of piety, and deliver us from this tempest. Let the good message of the Fathers be spoken by you in all liberty, destroying the odious heresy of Arius and building up the Churches in the salutary doctrine which professes that the Son is consubstantial with the Father [ὁμοούσιος] and that the Holy Spirit is equally honored [ὁμοτίμως] and adored with them [συλλατρεύεται]. Thus this liberty of speech which the Lord gave you for the truth, and this glorying in the saving Trinity, God will grant them also to us, through your prayers and your assistance.

Letter 92 (not given) written in 372, resumes the argument of the preceding letters unto making real the universality of Nicene Orthodoxy in spite of the split between the two halves of Christendom, which was due to distance and to the growing polarization of two idioms and two cultures, Greek and Latin. It is prefaced by a list of thirty-two Eastern Orthodox bishops from Asia Minor and Syria who joined Basil voluntarily in sending a collective letter to the Westerners in favor of the unity of the Church.

BASIL, LETTER 203, TO WESTERN BISHOPS ON THE
SEACOAST (παραλίωταις), written in 375

Let not yourselves be caught by the following sophism: "We who inhabit the seacoast are out of reach of the ills which affect many, and we have no need to be helped by others. What, then, would be our benefit in a communion with others?" Indeed, the Lord has put the sea to separate the isles from the mainland, but he has united the inhabitants of the isles and of the mainland by charity. Nothing separates us from one another, brethren, unless we submit voluntarily to separation. We have one Lord, one faith, one hope. If you regard yourselves as the head of the Church Universal, the head cannot say to the feet: "I do not need you." If you range yourselves in another class of members of the Church, you cannot say to us who are ranged in the same body: "We do not need you." The hands are in need of each other, the feet make each other steady, and the eyes see clearly when they are both in focus. As for us, we recognize our weakness and crave to be in accord with you. For we know that though not present bodily you will greatly help us by your prayers in the most critical moments. It is neither fitting in the eyes of men nor pleasing to God that you should use the very words which even the people who know not God would not use; for these people, we hear, even those who inhabit self-sufficient lands, are eager to contract an alliance among themselves, were it only because of the uncertain future, and abide in their mutual deals, seeing they are profitable. And we, whose fathers resolved that by means of small characters the symbols of our mutual relationship would travel from one end of the earth to the other, and that we should all be fellow-citizens and kinfolks, we would now withdraw from the *oikoumenè* and not be ashamed of our seclusion! Do we not see that breaking the concord is fatal? Do we not shudder to become the object of the frightful prophecy of the Lord: "Because iniquity has increased, the charity of the greater number shall wax cold" [Mt 24:12]?

BASIL TO BISHOP AMBROSE, LETTER 197 (375)

Ambrose, prefect of Milan, called to the episcopacy by popular acclamation after the death of the Arian bishop Auxentius, occupied the metropolitan see of Lombardy, 374-397, fighting attempts at a revival of paganism and the spread of the Arian heresy in the West.

Great and numerous are the gifts of our Master, and it is impossible to measure the magnitude or the great number of those gifts. But one of the greatest gifts, if one appraises the graces we have received, is that we are able to communicate among each other, in spite of the great distance that separates us, by our exchange of letters, for God has gratified us in two ways: meeting together or conversing by letters. Therefore, because we have known you by the words you have spoken, because we know you, not by the physical character which we have carved in your memory, but by considering the beauty of the inner man, from the variety of your utterances—for each one of us speaks from the abundance of his heart [Mt 12:34]—we give glory to our God who chooses in every generation those men who are well-pleasing to Him. . . . Go then, O man of God, for you have not received or learned the Evangel of Christ from men, but the Lord Himself has taken you from among the judges of this earth and placed you on the seat of the Apostles; fight the good fight [2 Tm 4:7]; heal the infirmities of the people, if by misfortune they have been infected by the ills of Arian folly; retrace the former footsteps of the Fathers and, by the love you have for us, build on the foundation which you have cast, through the continuous greetings you shall send us! In that way we will be able to remain close to each other in spirit, in spite of the distance that separates our earthly abodes.

Letter 243 is Basil's appeal to the bishops in the Occident, to keep or renew contacts and make a common front against the spread of the Arian heresy or against the intrigants who threatened to wreck eastern Churches, under emperors hostile to Nicene Orthodoxy. Letter 92 (not given here), written four years earlier and signed by thirty-two bishops from Cappadocia, Armenia, and Syria, most of whom have not been identified with certainty, is a similar appeal to the Italians and Gauls.

BASIL TO THE BISHOPS OF ITALY AND GAUL, LETTER 243 (376)

To the brethren truly beloved of God and most desired, our concelebrants [συλλειτουργοῖς] who are of one soul with us, to the bishops of Gaul and Italy, Basil, bishop of Caesaraea of Cappadocia. Our Lord Jesus Christ, who has deigned to call the entire Church "his own body" and who has admitted each one of us as members, has given us also to be in harmonious intimacy all unto all as members should. For this reason, although we are separated from one another by the distance between our homes, we are close to one another, considering our union. . . . You will sympathize with the afflictions unto which we have been delivered because of our sins, and we shall rejoice all the more with you for the glorious peace which the Lord gave you. Already several times we have appealed to your love, for help and sympathy, but since our chastisement was not made full, you were not permitted to stand up to succor us. We seek above all that the ruler who reigns over your land be enlightened by your piety on our disorders, and if this is too difficult a task, we pray that some of your people come to visit and comfort the afflicted ones and have under their eyes the misery of the East. This misery your ears cannot perceive, because no words can be found to make you see clearly our condition.

A persecution has raged over us, most venerable brethren, and of all persecutions the most cruel. The shepherds are banished and the flocks shattered. And here is the worst: while those who are mistreated accept their sufferings in the certainty of martyrdom, yet the people do not range these athletes among the martyrs, because their persecutors assume for themselves the name of Christians. Nowadays there is only one crime that is punished most harshly, to wit: a scrupulous faithfulness to the traditions of the Fathers. For this reason pious men are exiled from the land of their ancestors and emigrate to desert places. . . . No evildoer should be condemned without proof, but some bishops have been convicted and tortured while no proof whatever was brought in support of the accusations. Some of them did not even know who their accusers were; they saw no court of law. It is not even upon the word of calumniators that they were condemned; yet, they were violently abducted at impossible hours of the night, exiled into foreign lands, and exposed to die, being left to suffer in desert places. What follows is known to everyone, even if we keep silence: the exile of priests, the exile of deacons, the enslaving of the entire clergy. . . . Do not consider only your own situation, that you lay at anchor in safe harbors because the grace of God has provided you with a shelter from the windstorms of this perversity. But do stretch your hands to the churches beaten by the tempests, lest they succumb some day in the shipwreck of the faith for having been abandoned. Weep on us, because the Only-begotten Son is blasphemed, and there is none to contradict. The Holy Spirit is rejected, and anyone who could refute the impious is exiled. Polytheism has prevailed. There is among those people a great god and a lesser god; they do not regard "the Son" as the proper noun of a nature [φύσεως ὄνομα], but as a common noun. The Holy Spirit does not close the circle of the Holy Trinity for them; it partakes not of the divine and blessed nature, but it is added to the Father and the Son, perchance and haphazardly, as something from the world of creatures. They feed impious doctrines to the churches' little children, and what will they do? Their baptisms, their rites for the dead, their visitations of the sick, their comforting those who mourn, their relieving those who are oppressed, their many helps, their partaking of the mysteries, all these acts, being performed by these people, turn into fetters binding people to the heretics. Still a little time, and even if there is some freedom left, there will be no hope any more that those who will have been for so long prisoners of imposture might again be reclaimed unto the acknowledgement of the truth.

The following three letters (195, 227, and 228), all written in 375, that is some five years after Basil's elevation to the metropolitan see of Caesaraea, show his concern for the welfare of the Orthodox in Armenia. He thought of visiting his friend Euphronios, the bishop of Colonia in Lesser Armenia, in spite of his failing health; it meant a voyage on inexistant or next-to-impassable roads. Euphronios was to be canonically transferred to the more important see of Nicopolis, and the prospect of this move met with a considerable emotion on the part of the Colonians, who planned to bring their grievance before the courts. This would have accomplished nothing, but would not have failed to indispose the authorities and serve the evil designs of politicoes who had set the entire Asia Minor and Syria into utter confusion, as many orthodox bishops were driven out of their Churches and sent into exile. For the time being Basil, whose personal authority overawed even the heretics, would advise Euphronios by letters, provided he could find reliable messengers to whom they might be entrusted. Letters 229 and 230, not given here, close the series; Basil exhorts the clerics and the magistrates of Nicopolis to cooperate with him in his efforts to pacify the Colonians, lest inconsiderate comments or rash decisions exacerbate their resentment at losing their pastor.

BASIL TO EUPHRONIOS, BISHOP OF COLONIA IN ARMENIA. LETTER 195 (375)

Colonia, which the Lord gave you that you would govern the Church, is at a great distance from localities served by roads. That is why, even if we write to our other brethren in Lesser Armenia, we hesitate to send letters to Your Piety, despairing to have someone who could carry them into such far-away places. We hope now that you will come in person, or that our letter will be delivered unto you by the bishops to whom we have entrusted it. So we are writing to Your Piety and we greet you by letter. We let you know that apparently we are still on this earth, and we beg you to pray for us, that the Lord would allay our sufferings and remove from us, like a passing cloud, the burden of pain which weighs our heart down. And so it shall be, if the Lord grants it to the most God-beloved bishops who are now in exile, being condemned for their piety, to come back soon.

BASIL TO THE CLERICS OF COLONIA, LETTER 227 (375)

Is there anything as beautiful and precious in the eyes of God and men as perfect charity? It is the fullness of the Law, as we have learned from our Master. Therefore we approve the ardor of your disposition toward your pastor. For a child who loves his father, to be deprived of him is unbearable; and for a church of Christ, the parting from a pastor and a teacher cannot be endured. It is the proof of a fair and right intention you give by your overwhelming affection for your bishop, and this happy disposition toward your spiritual father, kept within reasonable limits, is to be praised; if, however, it becomes excessive, it is no longer to be approved of. A right decision was taken with regard to our brother most beloved of God, Euphronios our concelebrant, by those unto whom the government of the Church has been entrusted; this decision was a necessary one in the actual situation, advantageous to the Church to which he was transferred and also to those from whom he was taken. Do not think that there is here a human maneuver or a calculation by earthly-minded men, but be assured that it was done by those upon whom the care of the churches belongs, with the assistance of the Spirit. Trust in the pending decision and implement it with zeal. Accept peacefully and with thanksgiving what has happened, and be sure of this: that those who do not accept resolutions taken for the churches by those whom God has chosen stand in opposition to God's order. Do not plead against your mother, the Church in Nicopolis. . . . One thing makes me very sad: it is that you said—and it seems to pass all measure—"If we do not get what we want, we shall have the courts compel them, and we shall manage to enlist men for whom the subversion of the churches is the supreme concern." Let not some fellows swept away by a mad fury persuade you to carry some of this affair before the public assembly; it would be catastrophic. Let the weight of the dissension fall back on the head of those who have been the cause of it. Receive the advice we give you with a fatherly heart and accept the decision of the bishops most beloved of God, to conform with God's will. Wait for our arrival. If the Lord grants us His help, whatever we could not demand by letter from Your Piety we shall recommend to you personally, and we will bring you by deeds the consolation which is in us to give.

BASIL TO THE MAGISTRATES OF COLONIA,
LETTER 228 (375)

I have received the letters of Your Excellencies, and I

gave thanks to the all-holy God that although you are kept
busy with the care of the public good you do not overlook
the affairs of the churches. Every one of you was concerned
with these affairs as with something on which his own life
depends, and you have written to us your grief at being
separated from your bishop most beloved of God, Euphronios. Now Nicopolis did not deprive you of him. The people
of Nicopolis argue that it is their own bishop they have actually received. The Church at Nicopolis will praise you with the
affection of a motherly love, for it shall share in common
with you a father who will bestow his grace in turn upon
each of you. God will not let the Colonians suffer from the
assaults of their adversaries, nor shall He rob you of his
customary protection. Think of the harshness of our time and
let a spirit of wisdom make you understand the necessity of
the resolution that was taken. Excuse the bishops who have
taken this measure for making stable the churches of Our
Lord Jesus Christ. Apply to yourselves the counsel that
belongs to men intimately acquainted with the situation,
meaning for the best and knowing also how to receive suggestions from those who love them. It may be that you do
not know many of the actual events, because of your location
at one extremity of Armenia; but we who are engaged in
the midst of affairs, we have our ears worn out every day
by ubiquitous rumors on the ruin of the churches and we
are in great perplexity. We fear that the common enemy,
envious of our life-long peace, may seed his tares even in
your regions and that the land of the Armenians may become
the prey of its adversaries. Somewhat later, if the Lord gives
us license to go to you, you shall receive more precise infor-
mation on the events, if you judge it necessary.

*Letter 85 illustrates an ethical problem on which Basil
advised a local representative of the civil power. He wrote
him a letter respectful but firm, to warn him against the
abuse of oaths imposed upon tax payers by fiscal agents.*

The title in the Greek manuscript reads that "one should not swear an oath," (περὶ τοῦ μὴ δεῖν ὅρκουν). The subject is for us of actuality, as the intricacies of tax returns and similar documents threaten to turn law-abiding citizens into crafty casuists or shameless liars.

BASIL, LETTER 85 (372)

We do not cease, in all our synods and our private conversations, to protest against tax collectors who ought not to impose upon country people the swearing of an oath for the payment of their taxes. It is still left for us to protest by letter, before God and men, regarding the same things. It is fitting that we should cease to bring death to the souls of men, and that we should figure out some other mode of taxation, permitting men to keep their souls from being wounded [by sin]. This we write to you, not because you need to be exhorted by words, for you possess at home every safeguard for fearing the Lord, but in order that those under you can learn through you not to provoke the Holy One, and not to regard such provocations an indifferent matter because of bad customs. The swearing of an oath is of no use for collecting taxes, and it causes men to admit into their soul an acknowledged evil. Once men have accustomed themselves to perjury, they are no longer in a hurry to acquit themselves of their debts, and they see in oaths a ready weapon of fraud and delay. And if the Lord would strike perjurors by His sharpest retributions, the tax collectors would have nobody any more to answer in the courts, because those liable to give account would have all perished under the chastisement. If the Master suffers in His longanimity, as I said before, that those who have experienced the kindness of the Lord still may disdain His goodness, let them not violate the law further with impunity and provoke God's wrath upon them-

selves! We have spoken the words pertaining to our office.
Those who will not listen shall see.

*Letter 31 was written when Basil, at that time a priest,
served on the staff of the archbishop of Caesaraea. There had
been a famine in Cappadocia and Basil was retained in the
metropolis for the organization of relief. He was sending in
his stead his blood relative Hypatios, who was ailing, and
whom he recommended to the charity and prayers of "the
brethren." Gregory of Nazianzus, in his funeral oration on
the death of Basil, relates how he had organized "popular
soups" for the victims of a famine.*

BASIL TO BISHOP EUSEBONAS, LETTER 31 (369)

The famine here has not yet eased, and our presence in
the city is necessary, either for the administration of the city,
or in our sympathy with those who suffer. That is why
I could not presently accompany our venerable brother Hypatios—my brother; this is not just a way of speaking, but because of our natural relationship, as we are of the same blood.
Your Excellency does not ignore what ails him. We deplore
that any hope of relief has been denied him, because those
who have the charism of healing could not possibly do anything through their customary skill. Here is why he requests
once more the help of your prayers. But now see to it that,
through your pity for the sick and through our intercession,
he may be comforted. If it is possible, call unto you the
most prudent of the brethren so that the proper attention be
given to him under your eyes; but if it is not possible, send
him with a letter and recommend him to the brethren, as
I have just mentioned.

There might have been some sort of understanding between the bishops and government officials for the relief of the many people in need of assistance. Intrigants and politicos were not making the task easier, and our churchmen had often to appeal to the common sense and conscience of civil functionaries to obtain some cooperation in granting reductions or exemptions from excessive taxes, imposed upon individuals or institutions by overzealous fiscal agents. Here again we find Basil in the lead, either before or after his elevation to the episcopacy. The following letters are addressed to civil officials, in favor of private persons or communities for whom our hierarchs requested an adjustment of state taxes.

SAINT BASIL TO A PROVINCIAL TREASURER,
LETTER 142 (373)

I had summoned our brothers the *chorepiscopoi* to the convocation in memory of Eupsychios [a victim of Emperor Julian], so that I might introduce them to Your Honor. But since you were absent, I have to present them by letter to Your Excellency. Be aware, according to your prudence, of the trustworthiness of this God-fearing brother [porter of the message]. Whatever he reports to your kindness toward the poor, give it preference as to one who is telling the truth, and do grant to the needy whatever assistance you can. You will naturally deign also to inspect the hospice of the poor in his resort and exempt it from all contributions. Your colleague has already agreed that the meager possessions of the poor should be exempt from taxes.

SAINT BASIL TO ANOTHER TREASURER,
LETTER 143 (373)

If I had been able to present myself personally to Your
Excellency, I would have made a complete list of matters I
wanted to treat, and I would have taken care of the poor, but
ill health and the hindrance of business have detained me.
I am sending in my stead, and I recommend to you this
brother, a *chorepiscopos,* so that you give him full attention
and consult with him as a lover of truth and a wise adviser
on business matters. If you deign to have a look at the
hospice of the poor [πτωχοτροφεῖον] which he administers
—you will do this, I am sure, and not just pass by, for you
are not ignorant of this business and, as I was told, you support the hospice of Amaseia with what the Lord gives you—
if, therefore, you see also his hospice, you will provide everything it needs. Your colleague has already promised to look
with interest after the hospices of the poor. I say this not in
order that you imitate him, since you are yourself unto others
a sure guide toward the good, but in order that you know
how others have already solicited me with regard to those
things.

*Letter 199 of Gregory of Nazianzus was written to en-
dorse the petition of Theodosios, director of an orphanage
(ὀρφανοτροφεῖον). It would be better to keep him in this
charge, rather than having him transferred to another post.*

GREGORY OF NAZIANZUS TO NEMESIOS, GOVERNOR
OF CAPPADOCIA, LETTER 199.
(written in Gregory's later years)

If I seem to be importunate with my frequent letters, do not wonder, or else I will charge you before the just judge—which you are—and I know you will acquit me. You are responsible for my daring because of your readiness to grant motions submitted to you, and no wonder! Many are the reasons for readily granting the favor I beg from you: my advanced age, my ill health, our common love of the *belles lettres*—if I may be counted among the *literati*—my desire to meet you, and the infirmities that hinder me from attaining that goal. But what is my request? If it were not right, it would make me ashamed to apply; if it is right, be ready to grant it. Our son most desired, Theodosius, appeals once more to Your Prudence; he is both yours and mine: mine as a "supervisor" [σκοπός, text uncertain], yours as a petitioner. He comes as a petitioner in a cause of mercy. Orphans are in danger, human beings are at stake, one does not know how it will all turn out. We apprehend the transfer of a father who has helped many orphaned children in need. Grant one single favor to all! Stretch your hand to a misfortune which you will appreciate yourself! You need not increase in glory, being in your charge, no more than Ἑωσφόρος, the brightest Morning Star! But if you still seek some increment, nothing can be better, know it well, nor shine brighter than the present occasion, ts many truthful men will tell Your Nobility.

Not all civil servants were cooperative. Basil wrote to Ilias, the eparch, who had some qualms about expenses involved in the building project of Basil and his collaborators: a church center, a combination hospital-hospice for the poor, a hostelry for travelers, all deemed too costly.

BASIL TO ILIAS, ARCHON OF THE EPARCHY,
LETTER 94 (372)

I wanted to meet personally with Your Excellency lest
I be forestalled by those who calumniate me, but I was
hindered by a bodily weakness which afflicted me more
cruelly than usual, and I had to write to you instead. . . . I
thought that our great emperor, having learned of our problems, had permitted us to administer the churches ourselves.
But those who harass your impartial ears, I would like that
they be asked in what the public good suffers on our account,
or which common interest, small or big, is being wronged
by our administration of the churches, unless one says that
damage is done to the republic if a house of prayers of a
noble structure is built unto our God, and around its
dwellings, a large residence for the presiding bishop [κορυ-
φαίῳ], and another one of lesser elevation, distributed in
apartments for those in charge of the divine office, and of
which you, the *archontes,* shall have free disposition with
your retinue. Whom will we wrong if we build rest houses
[καταγώγια] for the foreigners, occasional travelers as
well as persons in ill health who need to be taken care of,
and of establishing whatever is necessary for their relief,
medics, physicians, pack animals [νωτοφόρα], and convoy
personnel [παραπέμποντας]? It would be also necessary
to add arts and crafts, those that are needed for life, and
those that have been invented in order to ensure a gracious
living; and again, other houses suitable for working, all
things which are an adornment to the place and would be
an object of pride to our *archôn,* for the praise returns to him.

*The addressee of Basil's letter 88, probably the provin-
cial governor, was not identified in the earlier editions. The
title given by the Greek manuscript reads: "An epigraph,*

concerning a collector of revenues." The eastern provinces
of the empire were taxed in gold for the purchase of military
equipment; the bullion thus collected was to be deposited
in the treasury not later than April 1. Basil writes on behalf
of the citizens of Caesaraea, who found themselves unable
to meet their obligation in time, and suggests a postponement
of the date due.

SAINT BASIL, LETTER 88 (March 372)

The difficulty to collect the gold bullion Your Excellency
knows better than anyone else, and we have no better witness
of our own indigence than yourself, who in your great humanity [φιλανθρωπία] had compassion with us, and to this day
assisted and sustained us, never relaxing your kindness, for
fear that your conscience be disturbed from on high. There
is still, after our announcement, a small amount of gold to
be paid by the entire city. We beg from your consideration
to postpone somewhat the date due, so that those living outside the city might be notified, for most of the collectors
reside in the countryside, as you know yourself. If it were
possible that we send the contribution minus a few pounds—
this is the point of our request—the remainder would be sent
later. But if it is necessary that the payment to the treasury
be made as a single sum, let the date be deferred, as we have
just suggested.

*Basil, in letter 110, asks for some relief from the heavy
taxes on iron, imposed upon the inhabitants of the Taurus
districts. He had wished he could write to the prefect Modestos, but did not dare. This Modestos seems to have been*

*rather unapproachable, if we judge from the long preamble
and the unusual number of oratorical precautions Basil takes
before coming to the point of his request.*

Saint Basil to the Eparch Modestos, Letter 110 (372)

As much as you grant us of honor and freedom of speech
thanks to your kind condescension toward us, so much and
much more do we pray our good Master to increase your
prestige! For a long time I have desired to write to you and
benefit by your outstanding renown, but I restrained myself
by respect for Your Excellency, heedful of not going beyond
the permissible limits of free speech. But now, since your
peerless magnanimity gave me license, I make bold to write,
as the need of downtrodden people moves me. If there is
some power in the prayers of small folk to men of elevated
rank, grant us, O admirable man, that we may ask you the
favor of a humane decision for wretched peasants, in order
that the taxes on iron be more bearable for the inhabitants
of the Taurus, that region which produces iron, so that they
may not be crushed once and for all, but be preserved for
common utility which, we are convinced, is the greatest concern of your admirable philanthropy.

*By common usage, priests and clerical persons were
exempt from the general charges to the imperial treasury.
The fiscal agents, however, having bought their charge, were
naturally eager to recoup what they regarded as an advance
to the State, and tended to ignore the privilege of clerics.
Hence a number of petitions addressed by the bishops in*

favor of their priests to obtain from the authority a revision of their case and eventually a redress.

Basil, still a simple priest, had requested from an influential friend some assistance on behalf of a country priest with whom he had been brought up as a child. The tone of the note, almost negligently written, contrasts with the formal letters he sent to high-placed officials after his own elevation to the episcopacy.

SAINT BASIL, LETTER 36
(an epigraph of uncertain date)

The priest of that locality is known to your generosity for a long time, for he had been brought up with me. Is there anything more I might do but urge you to review his case favorably and help him with his problems? If you love me, as indeed you do, it is clear that you wish to help with all your power those whom I hold as second selves of mine. Now what am I asking for? That the former taxes of this priest be kept without augmentation; for he has not spared his good offices toward our subsistence, since—you know it yourself—we possess nothing and content ourselves with the resources of our friends and relatives. Regard the house of our brother as *my* house, or rather *your* house. God, for your kindness toward him, shall reward you, your house, and all your people. Know that I am quite determined that such an assimilation [*his, your,* and *my* house] will not prove insulting to our man.

SAINT BASIL TO THE EPARCH MODESTOS, LETTER 104 (372)

The very fact of writing to a man of your condition, even if there is no other reason, brings the greatest honor to those who write, since conversing with pre-eminent men brings renown to those who are deemed worthy. While struggling for my entire country, I have to present to Your Magnanimity the request through which I entreat you to receive me with your customary benignity, and to extend your hand to your country now falling on its knees.

Here is the object of my petition. The ancient census had exempted from taxes men consecrated to God: priests and deacons. But now the assessors, as if they had received no authoritative instruction from you, did assess them, with the exception of a few who were exempt anyway by reason of their age. We beg that at least the same exemption be granted as a monument of your kindness for all time to come, that we may help you remember. Grant, then, that the ministers in sacred orders be treated according to the older system of taxation, lest the exemption become a personal favor to those presently inscribed, for in that case the benefit might pass on to their heirs, and such people are not always worthy of the ministry! In accordance with the formula of free inscription, there ought to be a sort of clergy exemption, so that those in charge of the church taxes would exempt at each time the clerics who serve at the altar.

Saint Gregory, in letter 98, writes to the assessors of public revenue on behalf of a poor churchman in charge of a shrine dedicated to the martyrs, probably the Forty Martyrs of Sebastaea (Sivas). He enumerates the titles of that cleric, a certain Theoteknos (not to be confused with the layman of letter 78), for a reduction of taxes.

GREGORY OF NAZIANZUS TO THE ADMINISTRATORS
OF THE TOWN OF NAZIANZUS, LETTER 98
(date uncertain, before his retirement)

It seems to me that if you cut in two the duffel bag of
Diogenes and lay your hands on Diogenes himself, counting
as a valuable asset his cloak, his staff, his flight from all
possessions under pretense of philosophy, his loitering from
door to door, his happy-go-lucky living, just as it happens—
it all looks just as when you pretend to levy a tax on the
earnings of brother Theoteknos. What shall I say first, or
what is essential for his justification? That he is a deacon,
that he is poor, a foreigner, that he converses with other
people rather than with us, that his life is respectable, that
he is in sacred orders, serving at the shrine of the martyrs
and dwelling at their threshold? Know also that he practices
hospitality above his means; he is wrong only because, alone
among the people of your region, he forces them to be
honest. But what is the most important of all these things?
It is up to you to decide! For those reasons spare him,
strike a compromise with him and do not take the decision
of procuring a shabby advantage for the public treasury
at your own great detriment, by refusing to "clothe him
who is naked," as it is said, but by stripping him.

*Gregory (letter 211) writes to Kyriakos, a provincial
magistrate, to obtain an exoneration from real estate taxes
in favor of Sakerdos, a brother in the priesthood, who is
administering an important home for poor people.*

GREGORY OF NAZIANZUS TO KYRIAKOS, LETTER 211
(in Gregory's later years)

You honor pious men, I know, and you do good for
the poor. Here is a proper occasion on both counts. How?
Our reverend and most beloved of God, Sakerdos, our
brother in the priesthood, directs a well-known house for
the poor [πτωχεῖον], being prompted by piety and zeal
for his work. Among the premises of the house are the
domains of Liandros and Kaberina, contiguous to the
grounds of the asylum; they come from a donation made
by the most honorable Kastôr to provide for the mainte-
nance of the house. If you exempt those domains from
taxation altogether, you will ensure not a mean part of
those poor people's subsistence and earn for yourself the
reward that you know is due to pious men. It is obvious
that through this favor you will also provide for future
needs, by means of any procedure you may devise, and
restrain anyone attempting an action prejudicial to these
domains.

*Gregory requests from Hellebikhos, a high ranking offi-
cer in the imperial forces in the Orient, to give a proper
release to a certain Mamas who serves in the army, though
he had been tonsured as a church reader.*

GREGORY OF NAZIANZUS, TO HELLEBIKHOS,
LETTER 225 (written after 383)

How does ill health aggravate us! We should have

rushed toward you to embrace you in remembrance of our old friendship and intimacy, but our ailing body does not permit it. So we address you by letter: greetings and amicable salutation! As a gift for both of us, here is what we propose: Mamas, a church reader [ἀναγνώστης], the son of a soldier, has been consecrated to God on account of his good character. Discharge him for God's sake and for us; do not count him among the deserters and give him a proper discharge in writing, that he be not slandered by others. Thus shall you expect success for the war pursuits under your command. Those who have in hand the supreme power and a discretionary authority should have all the more regard for God, and thus put their hope [in Him].

Cappadocia, like any other province of the empire, had its share of common crimes: thefts, frauds and swindles, murders, assaults, abductions and rapes, whose perpetrators had to be brought before competent courts of justice and had submitted to canonical procedures for the application of what the former Codex Iuris Canonici *used to call "medicinal pains." We should remember that the Christians were only a part of the population and that Christians were divided among themselves. This complicated singularly the administration of justice in the empire. Conflicts of jurisdiction were unavoidable and at best were resolved by mutual agreement between secular and ecclesiastical judges. The following two letters show Saint Basil's view on how to treat criminals guilty of violent revolt and theft. Callisthenes, a magistrate, had called Basil to arbitrate the case of his house slaves, who were in revolt. Basil recommends that the course of justice be tempered by indulgence. He would have preferred to have the culprits brought before his metropolitan court, but agrees to their being deferred to the criminal court of Sasima, where the disorder has taken place.*

BASIL TO CALLISTHENES, ON A SACRILEGEOUS THEFT, LETTER 73

. . . That a man inflamed, angry, and ready to chastise those who have injured him would refrain from anger and restrain the full strength of his wrath to make us arbiters of the case, is something that gives us the great joy of finding him a spiritual son. Considering which, what is left but praying for your prosperity? . . . Since you have ordered that those revolted slaves be brought to the place where they have caused mischief, I would like to learn what your kindness intends to do. If you appear in person to require the punishment for their insolence, the slaves will be there; for what else shall be done but that which you decide? Only we shall no longer know what grace we have received, if we are not able to free slaves from torture. Should you be held back by the hazards of the road, who is going to take charge of these men? Who is going to punish them for you? If you direct that they appear before you, and if it is decided at all, then order that the judgment be held at Sasima, and show your own mildness of character and your magnanimity. Taking in hand those who have provoked you, having by this shown your dignity, dismiss them scot-free, as we have implored you in former letters, granting us the grace we ask for, and you shall receive from God the recompense for your act.

The addressee of letter 286 is a public official, not otherwise identified. The object of this letter, written in the time of Basil's episcopacy, is a case of theft, aggravated by the fact that it was committed in a church building, where used clothing was stored for distribution to the poor.

BASIL TO COMMENTARESIOS, LETTER 286
(date uncertain)

The professional thieves who stole, against the precept of the Lord, the coarse clothes of the poor who should rather be clothed than robbed, have been caught in this church [σύνοδος, literally: meeting house]. They have been arrested by those in charge of the policing of the church. But you thought that, since you administered the public affairs, it belonged to you to deal with these sorts of things. This is why I write to you that delicts committed in churches must receive from us the appropriate redress, and that the public judges should not be bothered with these matters. Therefore the stolen clothes which are in your custody, as is shown by your record and the copy made thereof in presence of all the assistants, I have ordered to be collected, part of them for the poor who may appear later, and part to be distributed among those present. As for the culprits, I have decided that they should be made to repent through instruction and in the knowledge of the Lord, hoping that, in God's name, I shall make them better for the future. The lashings ordered by the courts do not work, but we know that frequently the fearful judgments of the Lord set those men aright. Now, if you feel that you should refer them to the court, we have full confidence in justice itself and in the righteousness of man, to let you act as you choose.

Several letters of Basil to Amphilochios, the bishop of Iconium in Pisidia, constitute a running commentary on the canonical legislation of the time and would deserve a special study which my lack of competence in matters of Canon Law does not allow me profitably to undertake. I will content myself with selecting a few pieces from the letters of Amphilochios περὶ κανόνων *and other miscellaneous let-*

*ters which may be of interest to twentieth-century Amer-
icans, confronted as they are with unsavory social and
ethical problems.*

BASIL TO AMPHILOCHIOS, ON THE CANONS.
LETTER 188 (374)

. . . The woman who destroys voluntarily a fetus incurs
the pain of murder. There is with us no inquiring whether
the fetus was formed or not. In these matters, justice is
demanded not only for the child that was to be born, but
also against her who has schemed against herself, since
most of the time women die in these circumstances. To
this is added the destruction of the fetus, just another
murder, in the intention of those who dare to commit this
sin. However the penance of these women should not be
drawn out until their death, but they must accept the stated
term of ten years. The healing is not a matter of time, but
according to the manner of their repentance.

BASIL TO AMPHILOCHIOS, ON THE CANONS.
LETTER 199 (375)

. . . Those who have acquired their wives by rape, if
they were abducted after having been already promised to
others, those men [the rapists] must not be admitted [into
the church] until the woman has been taken away and
brought back under the authority of him to whom she

had been first betrothed, whether he is willing to receive her or repudiates her. . . .

If anyone takes for his wife a woman who is not free, she should be abducted and brought back to her relatives, either her parents or her brothers or any other natural protectors of the girl. If they agree to give her to the suitor, let the marriage take place; but if they refuse, they should not be forced.

As for the one who has seduced a woman, whether stealthily or by violence, he must be submitted to the penalty stated for fornicators. The penance fixed for fornicators is four years: during the first year they are rejected from the prayers of the church and must mourn before the entrance door; the second year they may be admitted to hear the lessons [of Scripture]; the third year, to penitence; the fourth year, they are allowed to consort with the people, but may not take part in the oblation [προσφορὰ]. Only afterwards can they be admitted to the full communion of the "holy gift," the Eucharist [κοινωνία τοῦ ἀγαθοῦ].

Letter 270, whose addressee seems to be a local priest or the village archôn, shows Basil's vigorous implementation of the principles exposed in the letters to Amphilochios of Iconium on the disciplinary canons. The crime of rape seems to have been a rather common occurrence.

BASIL, LETTER 270,
an epigraph (after 375)

I am most saddened by finding you not in anger, either overlooking what is forbidden or showing yourself incapa-

ble of realizing that the present case is a crime against
human life itself and against humanity, as well as an outrage
to free men. I am sure that if you had all been of this
opinion, nothing would have hindered this sort of evildoing
to be uprooted from our parts. So then, display in the
present case a truly Christian zeal and act in proportion to
the injury. The girl—no matter where you find her—use all
your energy to have her seized and brought back to her
parents. As for that fellow, exclude him from the common
prayers and publicly banish him. His accomplices—exclude
them too from the prayers with all their household for three
years, according to ancient canons. The village that has
received the seduced girl and kept her, even without forcibly confining her—exclude it altogether from the prayers,
in order that all learn to regard the abductor as a serpent
or any other wild beast to be chased, while his victim is to
be rescued.

*A letter of Basil, addressed in the early years of his
episcopacy to an unidentified priest, Gregory by name, gives
Basil's own views on the problem of the* virgines subintroductae. *This priest lived under the same roof with a woman
servant, perhaps a female relative or some "young niece,"
in violation of a canon of the Council of Nicaea prohibiting
the "introduction" of such persons into priestly households,
as had been customary in the early Syrian Church. See
Daniélou and Marrou,* The Christian Centuries: The First
Six Hundred Years. *New York (1964), p. 216.*

BASIL TO GREGORY, A PRIEST. LETTER 55
(From the early years of his episcopacy)

I have most patiently read your letters, and I wonder: you could plead your cause with us succinctly and easily by your acts, but you admit to continue in what is charged against you, and you try to heal with long words that which is incurable. We were not the first nor the only one, O Gregory, to decree that women should not dwell together with men. Read the disciplinary canon edicted by our holy fathers at the synod of Nicaea, which prohibits clearly that there be among us "introduced women" [συνει-σάκτους, *virgines subintroductae*]. Thus, if someone professes celibacy in words, yet acts as married men living together with their wives, it is clear that while he pursues the honor of a professed virginity he does not forsake an amenity which in his case is improper. You should therefore yield to our request, all the more easily that you say you are free from every carnal passion. I do not believe that a seventy-year-old man burns of passion for a woman, nor is it because of any impropriety that we have decided what we have decided, but because we have learned from the Apostle not "to put a stumbling block or hindrance in the way of a brother" [Rm 14:13]. We know that for some it leads to nothing objectionable, but it leads others to sin. Here is why we have ordered you, according to the decree of the holy fathers: separate yourself from this woman! And why do you accuse the *chorepiskopos,* remembering an ancient enmity? Why do you accuse us of having ears always ready to hear calumnies, instead of accusing yourself of not being able to deprive yourself of that woman's company? Drive her out of your house and place her in a nunnery, that she may be among virgins, and that your service be done by men, "lest the name of God be blasphemed because of you" [Rm 2:24]. As long as you continue acting as you did, the thousand and one things which you write in your letters will not help you, but you will die

empty and shall have to render account of your emptiness
to the Lord. And if you persist without correcting yourself,
you shall be anathema to all the people, and all who receive
you shall be excommunicated from the entire Church.

*Several points of church law regarding matrimony are
treated in Basil's letters to Amphilochios "on the canons."
Successive bigamy (the remarriage of a widower who has
lost his wife, or of a widow who has lost her husband) is to
be tolerated, though it is generally inadvisable; a third
union, though not invalid, would expose the spouses to a
severe penance.*

*We close this chapter with another point of church law
that can be of interest for a study of the notion of "econ-
omy,"* οἰκονομία. *Basil esteems that positive church rules
should* not *apply retrospectively to the activities of converted heretics or of catechumens prior to their being united
with the Orthodox Church, subject to a decision of the
hierarchy.*

BASIL, LETTER 199, ON THE CANONS (375)

. . . The women who were in the heresy and had professed virginity, while being in heresy, and later chose to
marry—I do not think they are to be condemned. Whatever
the Law says, it says it to those who are "under the Law"
[Rm 3:19]. Now those who were not yet subject to the yoke
of Christ were not aware of the rules of the Master. But
now they are acceptable to the Church and obtain by their
faith in Christ the remission of their sins, in addition to
being pardoned for the previous violations of His rules.

Generally no account should be demanded from the catechumens for their past activities. But, of course, the Church does not receive them without baptism; the prerogatives of "birth according to the Spirit" are most necessary for them.

7

Priests and Hierarchs: Upholders of Orthodoxy

Saint Athanasius and the Church fathers who were gathered at Nicaea (325) had laid down the foundations of the catholic dogma, which the major treatises written by the Three Hierarchs brought to completion in its structural integrity. But it is not these major treatises that are the object of the present chapter. They have been analyzed, scrutinized, and commented upon by successive generations of patristic scholars and theologians. We would rather scan the correspondence and personal testimony of our Hierarchs, as they invented and tested a theological language suitable for expressing in human terms the ineffable mystery of the Triune God.

The gradual elaboration of the dogma had as its complement the refutation of heretical theories, old and new, unremittingly reborn like the heads of some monstrous Hydra. Thus, in the wake of Arianism which had made deep inroads into the two halves of Christendom, heretical movements threatened the peace, as they were being exploited by political schemers eager to capture the favor of the basileus and his representatives. It is worth noting that Basil remained personally untouchable, so great was his popularity as archbishop of Caesaraea. A distinctive feature is that Basil thought it necessary to explain theological matters to non-theologians as well; he adapted his instruction to the capacity of his correspondents: pious women, *cultivated laymen, imperial functionaries, rhetors, and philosophers.*

With Basil's letter 263, to the Westerners, we enter into the quick of the subject: the exposition of Orthodox Faith and the refutation of heresies.

BASIL, TO THE WESTERNERS, LETTER 263 (377)

May the Lord our God, in whom we have hoped, favor you with the object of that hope and grant to every one of you a grace as great as the joy with which you have filled our hearts, a joy you gave us by the letters you sent through our most desired fellow priests and by sympathizing with us in our ordeals, for your compassion has made you "put on for us bowels of mercy," as those men have reported unto us. If our wounds remain the same, it gives us some relief to have physicians ready who could, given the occasion, bring a prompt remedy to our ills. . . . The impudence and shamelessness of the Arian heretics, after they had torn themselves openly from the body of the Church, continues but causes us little damage because their impiety is obvious to all. As for those who wrap themselves in sheeps' clothing, hiding behind a semblance of gentleness while in reality they tear pitilessly the flock of Christ, those people, I say, who come from among us, inflict easy damage to simple souls. . . . It is they who are dangerous and to be feared. . . . It is necessary to mention them by name, so that you know those who foment disorder among us, and that you denounce them clearly to your Churches. Our word is suspect to many, as if we were assuming an attitude of meanness on account of personal differences. You will obtain all the more credit in the eyes of those people, that your homes are further away; moreover, the grace of God will prompt you to care for those who are worn out, and if you are numerous enough to reach a decision by common accord, it is evident that your majority shall dispose everybody to adopt your conclusions without discussion.

Here is what could be done if you were willing to write to all the Churches in the East: if these forgers amend themselves, they could be admitted in our fellowship, but if they persist stubbornly in their novelties, we should separate ourselves from them. We do recognize that if we had been able to sit with you in your wisdom, we could have taken in common right decisions in these matters. But the time did not permit it, and to delay would be harmful, because the harm done by those impious men would have taken root. So we had to send to you some of our brethren as messengers; they will inform you of whatever we may have omitted in writing, and they will exhort Your Graces to procure to the Churches of God the assistance they are seeking.

Having pointed to the necessity of mentioning by name those who limped between heresy and strict Nicene orthodoxy, Basil was not long to pass to the act and named three of them: Eustathios of Sebastaea (Sivas) in Lesser Armenia, Apollinarios of Laodicaea (Latakia) in Syria, and Paulinus, a successor of Meletios on the throne of Antioch. Basil regarded them as questionable, for a variety of reasons.

Eustathios had been at first a disciple of Arius. Converted to the Orthodox faith, he was ordained a priest by bishop Hermogenes of Caesaraea, after whose death he was received by Eusebius of Caesaraea, an ardent defender of Orthodoxy. During his catholic phase, Eustathios, notable for his ascetic way of life, had become an intimate friend of Basil, who was soon to deplore Eustathios' fluctuations. Relapsing into heresy, Eustathios managed to conceal his "ungodly convictions." Imprudently promoted to the rank of bishop, he turned his coat once more and appeared to be the author of a pamphlet against the doctrine of con-

substantiality. Deposed from office, he maneuvered to be restored in his charge by a local council held at Tyana, in the Cappadocia Secunda.

Apollinarios was less of a chameleon. Basil had at first looked at him without disfavor, but was soon disillusioned. Apollinarios had found an expeditious way to cut short the discussions with the Arian leaders, but did away by the same token with the arguments of Nicene theology on the relation of the Persons to the divine Essence. In fact this tended to revive the old heresy of Sabellius interpreting the names of the three Persons in the Trinity as arbitrary designations of the Absolute Deity. But Apollinarios was a fast talker: "He writes too much," says Basil. Endowed with great facility, he was apt to state any thesis, and "he has filled the Universe with his lucubrations," heedless of the advice of one who said: "Beware of making many books!"

The third suspect denounced by Basil is Paulinus, who indeed professed the Nicene dogma still in its incipient stage of development. But Basil disapproved of his sympathy for the doubtful speculations of Marcellos of Ancyra (Ankara), for whom the Son did not exist in his own hypostasis nor the Holy Spirit in his particular one.

Of the three characters, Apollinarios fared the worst in Basil's eyes, who concluded his letter "to the Westerners" as follows:

Apollinarios has composed on the Resurrection some fabricated treatises, rather Judaizing, in which he says that we should return to the cult of the Law, again be circumcised, observe the sabbath and the dietary laws, sacrifice victims to God, worship in the Temple of Jerusalem; in short, from Christians we shall be turned into Jews. Is there not anything more ridiculous, or rather more alien to the doctrine of the Evangel?

Already in 375, after reminding the leading citizens of Neo-Caesaraea of his ancestral roots in the city, Basil had warned them against any attempts at reviving the error of Sabellianism. Here is the doctrinal part of letter 210, the beginning of which we have given in chapter 2, "Biographicals."

BASIL TO THE LEADING CITIZENS OF
NEO-CAESARAEA: LETTER 210 (375)

There are some among you who exert themselves at distorting the faith out of hatred for the dogma of the Apostles and of the Gospel, or of hatred for that truly great man Gregory [the Wonderworker] and his successors down to the blessed Mousonios [a bishop of Neo-Caesaraea], whose teaching is still ringing in your ears.

The error which Sabellius let loose and which the Fathers put down some people undertake to revive today and, for lack of proofs, forge dreams against us. Do part from these heads heavy with wine and vapors arising from drunkenness, pregnant with visions! We keep watch, for fear of God, we cannot keep silent. Learn from us, then, the damage which such people inflict upon you: Sabellianism *is* Judaism, and it infiltrates itself under the guise of Christianism into the proclamation of the Gospel. For he who says that the Father, the Son, and the Holy Spirit are one single reality under several persons [ἕν πρᾶγμαν πολυπρόσωπο] and professes only one hypostasis common to the three, what else does he do but deny the pre-existence of the Only-Begotten before all ages? He rejects also His sojourn and conversing with men, the descent into Hades, the Resurrection, the Judgment, and he denies the distinctive operation of the Spirit [τὰς ἰδιαζούσας ἐνεργείας τοῦ πνεύματος].

GREGORY OF NAZIANZUS, LETTER 125, TO
THE PREFECT OLYMPIOS (382)
(written shortly after Gregory's return from Constantinople)

Even a white head has to be taught, for old age, it seems
to me, is no proof of wisdom. At any rate I know better
than anyone else the intrigues and the impiety of the
Apollinarists; I have seen that their folly is unbearable, but
I thought that with patience it might still be possible to tame
them and to soften them little by little. It appears that I had
unwittingly made them worse and that I had harmed the
Church by my untimely philosophy of moderation, for it
has failed to put the wicked to shame. For the time being,
if I had been able to inform you personally of these things,
I would not have been slow in coming, know it well;
however, it was beyond my own power to bow down before
Your Excellency. But illness has driven me beyond that
point and the doctors prescribed a cure at the thermal
springs of Xanxaris [possibly *Kara-punar,* the "black
springs"], so I send this letter instead. They have dared,
these "wretches who will wretchedly perish" [Mt 21:41],
above their other mischiefs, to call in bishops deposed by
every synod in the East or in the West, and use the occasion
of their passage, exactly what for I cannot tell. They have
rebelled against all the imperial constitutions and against
your decrees, and they have bestowed the name of bishop
upon one of them, an impious fake. They have been thus
far encouraged, I think, by my "deadness," speaking literally. Now if this is bearable unto Your Constancy, we too
shall bear with it, as we had to do so often! But if it is
intolerable to our most pious *basileus,* then proceed against
them; your rigor will not possibly be equal to their folly.

The problem to be solved by the Orthodox of the fourth century was to define the relation of the ineffable Essence to the three divine Persons. Christian theologians faced a dilemma: tritheism, malignantly imputed to Basil, or the massive conception of a Superessence which reduced the divine Persons to being mere labels expressing the diversity of their operations. In other words the problem was to find a suitable terminology, which was further handicapped by the divergence of Latin and Greek semantics, and was liable to create ambiguities. Thus the term hypostasis (ὑπόστα-σις), which adds a technical precision to πρόσωπον (persona), parallels etymologically the terms sub- stance, sub- sistence, sup- positum, but substance and subsistence can also be said both of God's Essence and of the basis for the distinct activities of the Father, the Son, and the Holy Spirit. Basil never tired of repeating that hypostasis, the principle of subsistence which belongs properly to each of the divine Persons, is not the same thing as the Essence, οὐσία, which the Father, the Son, and the Spirit share in common. Basil is rightly credited with having coined the formula "one Essence, three hypostases" μία οὐσία τρεῖς ὑποστάσεις, which became the password of subsequent Orthodox triadology; it is inescapable, and has not been supplanted by any modern ideology; we can simply not accept being reduced to the pale deism of the Enlightenment. We cannot give up theology as a science having its own principles and its own methods.

The following letters are Basil's familiar expositions of his doctrine of the Trinity. The first one (letter 9) was addressed as early as 361-362 to a certain Maximos, a philosopher. Dionysios, in whose writings Basil and Maximos were particularly interested, is a third-century correspondent of another Dionysios, disciple of Origen and bishop of Alexandria (cf. Altaner, Patrologie, p. 140).

BASIL TO MAXIMOS, PHILOSOPHER, LETTER 9
(361 or 362)

Words are truly images of the soul. We have learned to
know you through your letters as, they say, one knows the
lion by his claws, and we are gratified not to have found you
lingering with regard to the first and greatest of goods,
namely the love of God and of the neighbor. We consider
these signs of your affability toward us and of your zeal for
knowledge. That everything is contained in those two, is
well known to every disciple of Christ. . . . The writings of
Dionysios which you were looking for have reached us, even
many of them, but not his books, and so we did not send
anything. As for our opinion, here it is! . . . In his zealous
refutation of the Lybian's impiety [Sabellius], he plunged
unconsciously into the opposite error by his craving for distinction. It would have been sufficient for him to show that
the Father and the Son are not identical with regard to the
subject [ὑποκειμένῳ], and he would have been victorious
against the blasphemer [Sabellius]. But this man Dionysios,
in order to prevail better and more fully, does not suppose
a mere otherness of the hypostases [ἑτερότητα τῶν ὑπο-
στάσεων], but a difference of Essence [οὐσίας διαφοράν],
a lesser power, and a disparity of glory. . . . With regard to
the Spirit, he uttered words that do not befit a spiritual man,
excluding the Spirit from the adoration of the divinity and
somehow demoting it, to be numbered among creatures made
to serve.

As for me, if I have to speak my mind, the expression
"similar in essence" [ὅμοιον κατ' οὐσίαν], once you add
the words "without difference," I accept as synonymous
with "consubstantial" [ὁμοουσίῳ], according to the normal
meaning of "consubstantial." That was what the Fathers of
Nicaea [325] had in mind when, having proclaimed the
only-begotten Son "Light of Light, true God of true God"
and similar designations, added "consubstantial" for a conclusion. It is impossible to imagine a difference between

light and light, truth and truth, the Essence [οὐσία] of the Only-Begotten and that of the Father. But if one does not add to the word "similar" [ὁμοίου], the words "without difference" [ἀπαράλλακτον]—that is just what they did in Constantinople [imperial synod, 359]—I am suspicious of the term "similar," because it detracts from the glory of the Only-Begotten, for we use often the word "similar" to signify a faint resemblance or a vague image of the model. This is why I accept the term "consubstantial" [ὁμοούσιον], for I believe that it is less open to misuse.

BASIL TO HIS BROTHER GREGORY, LETTER 38
(written toward the time of Gregory's elevation
to the See of Nyssa, 369-370)

Since many who write on the dogma of the mysterious Trinity make no distinction between Essence [οὐσία], an entity possessed in common, and the Hypostases [ὑποστά-σεις], they fall into the same error, speaking indifferently of Essence or Hypostasis: a few of them, accepting blindly this lack of distinctions, say that, since there is only one Essence, so there is also one Hypostasis; and conversely, those who profess three Hypostases, following the same line of reasoning, maintained three Essences in number. Because of this, and lest you suffer a similar misfortune, we have made a résumé of the problem. . . . We affirm this: That which is being said properly of one subject is indicated by the word "hypostasis." If I say "man," I am introducing into the ear of my auditors a somewhat indefinite signification of the word; on the one hand, the nature of "man" is what is being expressed, but on the other hand the actual reality of the subject proper is not signified. But if I say "Paul," I show the actual reality of the being that is expressed by the name. This is what "hypostasis" means, not the indefinite [ἀόριστος] notion "essence" [οὐσία], which finds no firmness because the reality it signifies is shared by several subjects; the "hypostasis" means this notion that defines and circumscribes whatever is common and imprecise in a given object, by means of its obvious properties. . . . So it is that the principle of the distinction that you have recognized with regard to "essence" and "hypostasis"—if you transpose it and apply it to the divine dogmas, you shall not fail. Whatever your mind suggests on the mode of being of the Father, even though our mind cannot fix itself on a distinct concept because we believe that the Father's being is beyond any conception, you shall think the same of the Son, as also of the Holy Spirit. The notion of "uncreated" and "incomprehensible" is one and the same for the Father and for the Son and for the Holy Spirit, since it is impossible that one be more uncreated or more incomprehensible and that another be less. We must have a clear conception of the Trinity by means of proper signs. We must distinguish that which is being considered common, as when we say "uncreated" or "incomprehensible" or any such qualifying word, and do not use those common notions, but distinguish that which is proper, using only those signs by which the concept of each Person is kept clearly apart, without being mixed with the consideration of the three Persons as a whole.

Letter 24 of Gregory of Nyssa, obviously posterior to Basil's letter 38, shows that Gregory had perfectly assimilated the teaching of Basil. He applies the triadology of his brother to the refutation and conviction of a certain Heraklianos, a heretic. Emphasis is laid on the distinction of the Divine Essence and the hypostases of the three Persons, and on the immediate connection of the Trinitarian dogma with the baptismal formula, a theme familiar to our three hierarchs.

GREGORY OF NYSSA TO HERAKLIANOS, A HERETIC, LETTER 24

The salutary doctrine of faith, when men receive in the simplicity of their heart the inspired word of God unto salvation, has its own virtue; it takes no particular ingenuity to seek confirmations upholding the truth since it is self-understandable and evident from the first moment it was delivered; namely, when we received from the Lord the words for baptismal regeneration and the mystery of salvation. For He said: "Go, teach all the nations, baptizing them in the name of the Father, and of the Son, and of the Holy Spirit, teaching them to observe all the things I commanded you!" [Mt 28:18-20]. Dividing Christian teaching into two parts, namely morals [τὸ ἠθικὸν] and formal dogmatics [ἀκρίβειαν], Christ established, on the one hand, the dogma of salvation on baptism and, on the other hand, He ordered that our life be directed by the distinction of the commandments. . . . For this reason, we advise those who are to work out their own salvation not to depart from the simplicity of the first principle of the faith, but to receive in their soul the Father, the Son, and the Holy Spirit, and not to imagine that these are just three different names for a single subject [ὑπόστασις]. For the Father cannot possibly be his own father, lest the appellation "the Son" begotten of the Father were not held as real; nor may one think that the Spirit is not one among the other two Persons. So he who hears is induced into the knowledge of the Father and the Son by the sole mention of the Spirit. We understand under each of these names the hypostasis properly and exclusively signified by the personal names: when we hear "the Father," we have heard the Cause of All; when we hear "the Son," we have learned the resplendent virtue of the First Cause unto the unification of the All; when we say "the Spirit," we mean the power that brings to completion everything that has been called into existence by the Father and the Son throughout creation. Thus the hypostases, according to the mode that

we have exposed, exist without confusion or separation
from each other—I mean the hypostases of the Father and
of the Son and of the Holy Spirit. But their Essence [οὐσία],
whatever it may be, since it is unutterable and incomprehensible, is by no means divided into several different na-
tures. Therefore, that which is inscrutable, incomprehensible,
not to be understood by reason, is the same in each person
of the Trinity, in whom we place our faith. If one asks what
the Father is by Essence [οὐσία], the right and true answer
is that it is beyond our understanding. In the same manner
the essence of the only-begotten Son cannot possibly be
comprehended by the mind, for it is said: "Who shall tell
his generation?" [Is 53:8; Ac 8:33]. And it is the same for
the Holy Spirit which, according to the word of the Lord, is
meant when He says: "You hear his voice; but where it
comes from and where it goes, you know not" [Jn 3:8].
Therefore we understand that there is no difference whatever
in the incomprehensibility of the three Persons [according
to the Essence], for none of them is more incomprehensible,
or less, than the other two. . . . And so we are baptized as
we were taught, into the Father, and the Son, and the Holy
Spirit; we believe as we have been baptized, for it is proper
that our confession be in unison with the faith; and we give
glory as we believe, for no human opinion may conflict with
the faith; and as we believe, so we glorify. . . . From the
[divine] operations [ἐνέργειαι] we learn the indivisibility
of the glory: "The Father gives life," as the Gospel says
[Jn 5:21]; the Son gives life, and also the Holy Spirit, according to the testimony of Him who speaks of "the life-
giving Spirit" [Jn 6:63]. We ought to know that the power
[to give life] originates in the Father, proceeds through the
Son, and is completed by the Holy Spirit, for we have learned
that all things are from God through the Son and subsist
in Him, that all are pervaded through the virtue of the Spirit,
and that all in all, things act according to His will, as the
Apostle says [cf. 1 Co 12:11].

BASIL, TO WOMEN LIVING UNDER A RELIGIOUS RULE
(κανονικαῖς), LETTER 52 (375)

. . . There have been some who said that the Son was
brought forth from non-being to being [Arius' basic propo-
sition]. In order to do away with this impious saying, the
fathers have added that the Father and the Son are ὁμοούσιος ["of the same essence"]; the union of the Son and
the Father is not bound to the course of time, but is eternal.
Furthermore the words that precede this assertion of the
creedal formulae show that such was the thought of these
men [the fathers]. When they said "Light of Light," or that
the Son was begotten "from the essence of the Father," [ἐκ
τῆς οὐσίας], not made, they added the words "of the same
essence," indicating that what is said of the Light with regard
to the Father would suit the Son just as well. Between "True
Light" and "True Light" there is no difference whatever,
according to the notion of light as such; the Father is light
unoriginated, the Son is light begotten; one is light, the other
is light also. Therefore the fathers rightly said "of the same
essence," in order to show their equal dignity of nature. . . .
    The Holy Spirit is counted together with the Father and
the Son because it is also above the creature, and it ranks
third, as we learned when the Lord said in the Gospel: "Go,
baptize in the name of the Father, and of the Son, and of
the Holy Spirit" [Mt 28:19]. Therefore he who places the
Holy Spirit before the Son or says that it is more ancient
than the Father, contradicts the divine order and strays from
sound faith because he does not keep the right mode of
glorification, but imagines for himself a new way of speaking, in order to please men; for if the Spirit is above God, it
is not from God, and yet it is written: "The Spirit is from
God" [1 Co 2:12]. But if it is from God, how can it be more
ancient than He from whom it is? What is that folly, to say
that there is one Holy Spirit above the only-begotten Son,
when there is only one unbegotten? The Holy Spirit is neither
before God's only Son [ὁ μονογενὴς] nor something be-

tween the Son and the Father. But if it is not from God, yet
through Christ [διὰ Χριστοῦ], then it is nothing at all. Such
an innovation about the order of the Persons is a negation
of the Spirit's very existence, a rejection of the entire faith,
and it is equally impious to lower the Holy Spirit to the level
of the creature, or to place it above the Son and the Father,
be it according to time or to order. These are the points on
which, I believe, Your Piety desired some clarification, and
if the Lord grants that we may come together, we will speak
more of these problems and reach with you a fuller understanding of what we are searching for.

BASIL TO COUNT TERENTIOS, LETTER 214 (375)

. . . "Hypostasis" and "Essence" [οὐσία] are not the
same thing, and even our brethren from the West, I believe,
have suggested it, distrusting the rigidity of their language,
when they translated the Greek noun οὐσία, so that if there
is some difference in the concepts, this difference ought to
be kept by means of a clear and neat distinction of names.
If we must expose our opinion briefly, we will say that
"Essence" is to "Hypostasis" as "common" is to "particular."
Each one of us partakes of being by the common notion of
"essence," but we are *this* man or *that* man by our own
individuality. Here also [namely in the Trinity], the concept
of Essence is common, as are goodness, divinity, and any
attributes, but the Hypostasis regards the proper character
of fatherhood, sonship, and sanctifying power. If one says
that the persons [τὰ πρόσωπα] are without Hypostasis, it
is a sheer absurdity, but if one agrees that the Persons exist
truly in their respective Hypostases, which we profess, he
will realize that the principle of "homo-ouseity" [ὁ τοῦ
ὁμοουσίου] must be maintained in the unity of the divinity—
and let the pious acknowledgement of the Father, Son, and

Holy Spirit be proclaimed in the perfect and integral Hypostasis of each of the Persons who are named.

In the preceding group of letters, we have been watching Basil in his search for a terminology to express the relationship of the divine Essence to the three personal Hypostases and the order of the Hypostases in the Trinity.

This doctrine of the Trinity engages the very catholicity of the Church Universal. The correspondence of our hierarchs shows how a complete accord was realized step by step, so to speak. Basil and Gregory of Nazianzus were in general agreement on the substance of the dogma, but did not necessarily see eye to eye on the strategy to be adopted for making it acceptable to their contemporaries. At times it was rough going! Sharp words were exchanged between the two friends, until good will and common sense prevailed. Gregory of Nazianzus' letter 58 describes a symposium which started the quarrel. Basil does not seem to have been overfond of "banquet theology."

GREGORY OF NAZIANZUS TO BASIL, LETTER 58

. . . I am going to tell you something that happened recently. There was a symposium attended by quite a few well-known people and by our friends. A fellow came with them, all wrapped up in the name and habit of piety, a monk! The drinking had not begun yet and, as may well happen in a symposium, the conversation turned upon us, fault of some other topic. They all admired you, extended their admiration to myself, talked about the philosophy we both share, of our friendship, of Athens, of our common aspirations and feelings.

But our philosopher disapproved mightily: "What are you saying there, you people?" And he exclaimed loudly, like a young fool would do: "Are you all so many liars and toadies? That these men may be approved of above the rest, as you please! I will not dispute that. But I will not concede the main point: in matters of theology, you are wrong in praising Basil, and wrong in praising Gregory. The one betrays faith by his arguments, the other by his complicity in what he allows to be said."

"Where did you get that from, you fool," I said, "new Dathan and Abiron by your vanity [Nb 16]? Whence do you come to us and lay down the dogma? How do you make yourself judge of such important questions?"

He replied: "I am just arriving from a reunion in honor of Eupsychios the martyr—now that was true—where I heard your famous Basil talking theology. Regarding the Father and the Son, it was excellent, it was perfect; nobody could have said it better. But the Spirit—he filched it away!" And the fellow added some comparison with rivers flowing among rocks and disappearing in the sand. "And why, O admirable man," he said, looking straight at me, "why do you assert now that the Spirit is God?" And he told how, speaking on theology in a numerous company, I had applied to the Spirit the well-known maxim of Scripture: "Till when will we hide the lamp under the bushel?" [Mt 5:15]. "Basil," he said, "gives only a glimpse and a rough sketch of the doctrine; he does not speak the truth openly. He is more political than pious, he saturates our ears and veils his duplicity by the power of his verb."

I answered: "I live rather withdrawn, unknown to many who do not even know what I say nor whether I am speaking, so I can philosophize with impunity. As for Basil, his words are more important, for he is conspicuous by reason of his personality and of his church. Everything he says in public makes him the object of passionate debates. The heretics lie in wait for some unguarded statement in order to lay their hands on him and chase him from his church, for he is the only spark of truth that is left and the sole power of life, while heresy has gotten hold of everything around. Thus evil would take root in the city [Caesaraea], be spurred on, and would overrun the entire world. It is better for me to expose the truth cautiously and give way somewhat in the present situation, like under a passing cloud, than to let truth go by default, under pretense of proclaiming it loudly. For me there is no harm in saying that the Spirit is God, by using other words conveying this assertion; truth is less in the sound of words than in the intended meaning. But there is a great loss for the Church if truth is driven away because of a single man."

The company did not accept this caution which they regarded as a bad joke on them. They cried out against me as if I preferred cowardice to doctrine. "It would be much better," they said, "to safeguard our people by truth, than losing them without winning the others, by a sham prudence!" . . .

As for you, my godly and dear friend [literally *dear head,* κεφαλή], teach us how far we may go in the theology of the Spirit, which terms we should use, what should be our measure of caution, so that we may master all these notions, over against our opponents. I know you better than anybody else, and while we give each other full confidence, I would be the most stupid and the most unfortunate of all men if I failed to do that.

Basil's letter 71 shows that he took amiss the polity of provisional moderation commended by Gregory according to the symposium. The chronology of the three letters, Gregory's 58, Basil's 71, and Gregory's 59, which belong together, fluctuates somewhat: between 371 (Courtonne) and 372-373 (Gallay). We shall not enter into the discussion of these dates, which are only approximate. Gregory hoped to win moderate Arians or wavering Orthodox and bring them to profess the divinity of the Holy Spirit on par with the divinity of the Father and the Son. This had not been explicitly defined by the Fathers of Nicaea; in fact, the original Nicene

Creed (325), after defining the consubstantiality of the Father and the Son and their mutual relationship, "light of light, true God of true God," stops abruptly: "and in the Holy Spirit." It would be left to the first Council of Constantinople (381), whose Creed we sing at the divine liturgy, to bring the theology of the Trinity to completion.

BASIL, LETTER 71, TO GREGORY OF NAZIANZUS

I have received the letter of Your Piety through the most excellent brother Hellenios, and the things you have related to us we have heard from him when he told them to us, the naked truth! What has been the disposition of our mind you cannot have the slightest doubt about. However, since we have decided to place our love for you above any disappointment, we have received the news and we pray to Holy God that, for the days or hours that are left to us, we may remain toward each other in the same disposition as formerly, having our conscience clear from any conflict, whether light or serious. That a fellow who not long ago placed his honor in spying upon the life of Christians and believed that by frequenting us he acquired a certain distinction, that such a fellow would construct what he has not heard and expound what he did not understand, is not extraordinary. But what is strange and unexpected is that he can find an audience for those utterances, namely, my most intimate friends among your brethren, and not only auditors but disciples, so it seems. . . . One cause for it all, and I had begged you to prevent it, is that we never come together. But out of weariness I hold my tongue! If we spent together a good part of the year, according to our former convention, and because of the solicitude we owe to the Churches, we would not leave the door open to calumniators. Dismiss them unceremoniously, but let me ask from you to pool our efforts in view of the present struggle and march together against that pugnacious fellow. Just show yourself and you will hold back his fury or thwart the conspiracy of those who aim at ruining the state of our country, as soon as you will make clear to them that, through the grace of God, it is you in person who will head our assembly, and so you will close every foul mouth uttering impious statements against God.

The discord did not last long. Remaining faithful to each other, Basil and Gregory had always kept their freedom of thought and speech. Gregory felt that he had unwittingly hurt his friend, and tried to make good for it by writing a note (letter 59)—rather clumsy—in order to apologize for his faux-pas.

GREGORY OF NAZIANZUS TO BASIL, LETTER 59

My letter saddened you, neither rightly nor justly, I should say, but certainly beyond measure. You did not admit this sadness, but you could not hide it from me, even if you did it cleverly, as if you covered your sadness bashfully with a mask. If I have behaved deceitfully and maliciously, I should be punished, less on account of your grief than by truth itself. But if I acted from simplicity and in good faith, as is proper, I shall blame my sinfulness, not your state of mind. Only it would have been better to straighten up things than to be vexed against those who give advice. You shall see for yourself, since you are able to advise the others in these matters. You will find me ready, God willing, to stand by you in combat and to support you to the most of my ability, for who would lose confidence and who would not speak and exact himself at your side for the sake of truth?

*The two friends were soon totally reconciled. Basil seems
to have invited Gregory, banished from his Church at Sasima,
to visit him or perhaps to join him at Caesaraea. But Gregory had to decline the invitation, for he had to assist his
mother Nonna on her sickbed; she was to die shortly thereafter.*

*We have already met the disquieting figure of Eustathios
of Sebastaea, whose asceticism had at first won the friendship
of Basil, until sharp differences on the theology of the Trinity
made them irreconcilable enemies. Basil's letter 233, to the
Westerners (377), branded Eustathios as totally unreliable
(see chapter 3). The following pieces from our file on Eustathios will expose his perpetual see-sawing between Nicene
Orthodoxy and Arianism.*

BASIL TO COUNT TERENTIOS, LETTER 99 (372)

Although I have put all my zeal to comply, at least in
part, with the imperial ordinance and with the friendly message of Your Merit, confident that all your reasons and your
decisions are full of right intentions and sense, my good will
was not allowed to pass to the act. . . . After we had been
invited to meet with our brother bishop Theodotos [of Nicopolis in Lesser Armenia], charity urged us to accept the
invitation, lest we would seem to render this reunion un-
profitable and useless, and we were eager to enter into conversation with our brother Eustathios [bishop of Sebastaea].
We exposed unto him the accusations regarding faith, which
brother Theodotos and his people bring against him, and
we asked him, if he followed the right faith, to make it clearly

known to us, so that we could be in communion with him; but if he was not so disposed, he should know for sure that we would not be well disposed toward him either! We talked a lot together and spent the day discussing these questions, and when the evening came we parted without having reached any accord. Again on the following day, in session since the morning, we discussed the same problem; brother Pimenios, the priest of Sebastaea, had arrived by then, and sustained heatedly a doctrine different from ours. Little by little we disposed of the objections that Eustathios had formulated, and we brought these men to agree with us, so that by the grace of God not the slightest variance could be found between us. Now, toward the ninth hour [ca. 3 p.m.], we stood up for the prayers, giving thanks to the Lord who had brought us to think and speak in the same way. After this I still had to obtain from our man [Eustathios] a written agreement, in order that his assent be evidence to his adversaries and serve as a sufficient proof of his dispositions to the others. I wanted myself, as I was conversing with the brethren in Theodotos' house, to obtain from them, for more precision, a written statement of faith which we would present to Eustathios. This would serve a double purpose: that he would make a profession of the Orthodox faith, and that they would be satisfied, because they would have no objections any more, once their proposition was accepted. . . . After which the time came when we had to leave for Greater Armenia. Since I knew the peculiar character of Eustathios, I wanted to have a trustworthy witness so that I could give my own account of what had been done; in the same time, it might satisfy our man. So I went to Getasa, the domain of the most beloved of God Meletios [a bishop in Lesser Armenia], where I met with the aforesaid Theodotos; he reproached us for consorting with Eustathios, but then I told how our interview had come out, and how I had made Eustathios agree with us on everything. Yet Theodotos affirmed that Eustathios had denied it after parting from us, and categorically affirmed to his own disciples that he did not agree with us at all regarding the faith. To which I replied—and here consider, O you the most admirable of men, if my retorts were not very right and undeniable—I replied that I was persuaded, judging from the constancy of the man [Eustathios] about everything else, that he would not so lightly turn round about; if he admitted something now, he would not deny it right away. . . . But if perchance the reports that you repeat are founded, we must present him with a written statement containing the full exposition of the right faith. If I find that he signs this statement, I shall remain in communion with him, but if I catch him shunning away, I will renounce his communion. My words being approved by Bishop Meletios and by brother Diodoros, our co-presbyter, who was present, the very reverend brother Theodotos gave his consent.

BASIL, LETTER 125: COPY OF THE PROFESSION
OF FAITH SUBMITTED BY BASIL AND
SIGNED BY EUSTATHIOS (373)

People who have been deceived by heterodoxy and have decided to revert to the unity of Orthodoxy, and those also who for the first time wish to be taught the doctrine of the Word of Truth must be instructed in the confession that has been written by the blessed Fathers who met at Nicaea. The same may prove useful also against people suspected to be opposed to the sound doctrine, and who conceal their corrupt theories under deceptive excuses; for them also, the present confession of faith itself will be sufficient. . . .

"We believe in one God, Father Almighty, maker of all things visible and invisible. And in one Lord Jesus Christ the son of God, the only-begotten [μονογενὴς] of the Father; that is, of the Essence [ἐκ τῆς οὐσίας] of the Father. God of God, Light of Light, true God of true God; begotten, not made; consubstantial [ὁμοούσιον] with the Father; by whom all things were made, those in heaven and those on earth. Who for us men and for our salvation came down and was incarnate; he was made man [ἐνανθρωπή-σαντα], has suffered, and was raised on the third day; He went up to heaven; He shall come to judge the quick and the dead. And in the Holy Spirit." As for those who say that there was [a time] when the Son of God was not, because he was not born of beings that existed not, and for those who say that he is of another hypostasis and another essence, pretending that he was subject to change or altera-tion, the catholic and apostolic Church anathematizes these people. . . . It is also necessary, with men who are heedless of themselves and do not envisage the inescapable threat with which Our Lord has threatened those who blaspheme the Holy Spirit, that we make this motion: Those saying that the Holy Spirit is a creature, are anathema; namely, those who think it, and do not profess that the Holy Spirit is holy by nature [φύσει], like the Father is holy by nature and the Son is holy by nature, and who ban the Holy Spirit from having part in the divine and blessed nature. The mark of Orthodoxy is that we do not separate the Spirit from the Father and the Son. We must be baptized as we have been taught, we must believe as we are baptized, and we give glory as we have believed, to the Father, the Son, and the Holy Spirit. Orthodoxy cuts from its communion those who call the Spirit a created thing, for they are manifest blas-phemers. A remark more is necessary, on account of calum-niators: it remains that the Holy Spirit is unbegotten, for we know only one Unbegotten Principle of all things, the Father of our Lord Jesus Christ; the Spirit also is unbegotten, for we have learned from the Tradition [παραδόσει] that there is only one *Monogenès;* we have been taught that the Spirit of Truth proceeds from the Father, and we profess that it is of God and uncreated. Anathema also on those who say that the Holy Spirit is a servant, because by this word they reduce it to the order of the creature, since Scripture has delivered unto us that the ministering spirits are creatures, when it says: "All the ministering servants are sent forth to serve" [Heb 1:14]. And because of those who mix every-thing and do not keep straight the teaching of the Gospels,

it is necessary to add this: one must flee those who fight
openly against piety by altering the order delivered unto
us by the Lord, and by placing the Son before the Father,
and the Holy Spirit before the Son. We ought to keep
immutable and inviolate the order we have received from
the mouth of the Lord when he said: "Go, teach all nations,
and baptize them in the name of the Father, of the Son, and
of the Holy Spirit" [Mt 28:19].

Signature of Eustathios, bishop.

I, Eustathios, having read this that is before you, Basil, do
acknowledge and approve the above statements together with
you. I have signed in the presence of the brethren, our
Phrontonos, the chorepiscopos Severus, and several other
clerics.

*In a letter written in the latter years of his life, Basil
congratulates and encourages the Evaisenians [Εὐαισηνοῖς]
who had not been misled by the dogmatic and political
vagaries of the time.*

BASIL TO THE EVAISENIANS, LETTER 251 (376)

A Church pure and untouched by the harshness of our
times is not easily found and from now on rarely to be seen
—a Church that has preserved the apostolic doctrine un-
adulterated and inviolate! . . . Beloved brethren, we are
small and humble, but we have not accommodated our faith
according to changing events. We do not have one faith in
Seleucia, another in Constantinople, another in Zélis, another in Lampsakè, and a different one for Rome. The faith

that is professed today is not different from the one that came before; it is the one and same faith. As we have learned from the Lord, so are we baptized; we are baptized as we believe; and as we believe, we glorify God. . . . Be firm in the faith; look around the world and realize how small the part is that is diseased. All the rest of the Church, which from one extremity to the other has received the Gospel, abides in sound and undeviating doctrine. We pray that we may not be cut from her communion and that we may have a part with you on the day of the Lord Jesus Christ, the day of Judgment, when He comes to render to each one of us according to his deeds.

Basil, writing to Optimos, a bishop who had consulted him on the meaning of Genesis 4:15, presents us with a sample of his exegesis. The letter makes a total abstraction of the controversies that were raging throughout the Churches of the East. Basil appears here not as the archbishop, but in the more humble role of a fourth-century professor of Old Testament, who had studied for some time at the schools of Caesaraea on the Sea which had been founded by Origen. The text to be explained is given, of course, according to the Septuagint. The Hebrew text, followed by the Latin Vulgate and the modern versions, is notably different; it reads: "If anyone slays Cain, vengeance shall be taken on him seven-fold" (RSV). Omnis qui occiderit Cain, septuplum punietur (Vulg.) As it reads, Basil's letter may serve as a conclusion for our collection of snapshots of the three hierarchs as teachers of the doctrine.

BASIL, LETTER 260, TO OPTIMOS, BISHOP (377)

... You have inquired about the meaning of this famous
saying which is repeated everywhere up and down: "Who-
ever kills Cain *shall nullify* seven acts of vengeance" [Gn
4:15, LXX: ἑπτὰ ἐκδικούμενα παραλύσει]. . . . These
words can be understood in a simple way according to the
obvious sense, but admit also another interpretation. The
easy meaning that comes to mind is that Cain must be punished seven times for his crimes. But it is not fitting that a
just judge should fix retributions merely on the basis of the
"this for that": the culprit who has given the example of sin
ought rather to repay his debt with usury, if he is to amend
himself through the inflicted penalties, and make other men
wiser by his example. Since it had been decided that Cain
should pay a sevenfold penalty, the man who would slay him,
says the Scripture, would nullify the judgment of God on
Cain. This is the meaning that comes to mind at a first
reading.

But diligent men set their minds to explore things in
depth; so they want to know how justice is satisfied by a
sevenfold penalty, what the penalties are if the crimes committed are seven in number, and whether there is one crime
and seven penalties for it? Scripture always fixes the number
seven as the limit for the remission of sins. "How many
times," it says, "will my brother sin against me and I shall
forgive him [Peter speaking to the Lord]; up to seven times?"
And the Lord answered: "I do not say seven times, but to
seven times seventy" [Mt 18:21-22]. The Lord did not
change the number but multiplied by seven for fixing the
limit of the remission. After seven years, the Hebrew slave
was to be freed [Dt 15:12]. In the old time, seven weeks of
years [namely 49 years +1] made up for the celebration of
the Jubilee, during which the earth kept the sabbath; debts
were remitted, slaves liberated [Lv 25:10]. It was the beginning of a new life cycle; the former one had found its completion in the number seven. These were the types of our

age which revolve through the seven days of the week, which govern us; in such periods, lighter sins are atoned for according to the indulgent solicitude of our good Lord, lest we be delivered to eternal punishment. The expression "seven times," therefore, was used because of its kinship with this world, so that secular-minded men should receive a punishment commensurate with their perversity. . . . As for the punishments, if you speak of the sins committed by Cain, you shall find seven of them; if you mean the penalties determined for him by the Judge, you shall not miss what is meant either. The first of Cain's sinful acts which he dared to commit is his jealousy toward Abel, because Abel had been preferred to him; the second is the knavish way in which he called his brother, saying: "Let us go to the fields!" [Gn 4:8]; the third is the murder, a more grievous evil; the fourth is that this murder is a fratricide, the worst crime; the fifth is that Cain, the first murderer, has left an example of wickedness to all men; the sixth is that he had plunged his parents into mourning; and the seventh that he lied to God, for when God asked: "Where is Abel thy brother?" he answered "I know not!" [Gn 4:9]. Thus there were seven motives for punishment with which Cain was charged.

. . . But now we asked whether the torments Cain had to endure were seven in number, and the answer is "Yes." In answer to the question of the Lord—"Where is Abel thy brother?"—it is not that the merciful Master wanted to learn anything; He wished to give Cain an occasion of repentance, and the text makes it plain: "The voice of the blood of thy brother cries unto me" [Gn 4:10]. . . . If Cain had been deprived of God's attention, he would have had a pretext, feeling himself forsaken and deprived of an opportunity to repent. But now the physician appears, so that the patient may have recourse in him. Yet the patient not only hides the wound, but adds another one by joining lies to murder: "I don't know! Am I the guardian of my brother?" [Gn 4:9].

Now, count the punishments: "The earth is cursed because of thee" [Gn 3:17], first punishment. "Till the earth" [Gn 4:17], second punishment. A secret necessity kept Cain under the yoke and forced him to till the ground so that he could not possibly have some rest; he would continue to suffer because now the earth is his enemy, whom he has defiled with the blood of his brother. "And the earth will not yield her strength any more" [Gn 4:12]. Since the toil is without end and since the earth is sterile, here is the third punishment, namely, the futility of labor. To those three penalties God added two new ones: a continuous groaning [fourth punishment], and a shaking of the body of Cain [fifth punishment], whose members were deprived of their vigor: "Thou shalt be moaning and shaking about the earth" [Gn 4:12]. There is still a penalty [the sixth one], which Cain himself reveals, saying: "If thou chasest me now from the earth, I shall hide myself from thy face" [Gn 4:14]. . . . For the wise, this is the most cruel punishment, to be separated from God! "But it will happen," says Cain, "that the first passer-by who finds me will kill me!" And what says the Lord? "Not so!" [Gn 4:15], and He put a mark on Cain. This is the seventh punishment, not the hidden one, but proclaimed unto all men as by a herald. Cain is branded with a visible sign as the author of his crimes.

8
Priests and Hierarchs: The Arian Persecution

In the preceding chapter, we tried to follow our hierarchs' refutation of heretical doctrines and their exposition of catholic dogma, as reflected in their correspondence. We will follow them now in the struggle against heretics and their allies in government circles. The Churches of the Middle East had been most severely affected under the reign of Emperor Valens (364-378). Valens was personally hostile to Nicene orthodoxy, and his provincial administrators followed suit. Heterodox and heretics were in the majority. The province had been divided into two eparchies, in itself a mere administrative move, but soon exploited by intrigants. Demosthenes, the imperial vicar sent to supervise the situation in Cappadocia, proved himself to be a rabid pro-Arian. Among other vexatious measures, he ordered the arrest and deportation of Gregory of Nyssa. Basil's protest in letter 225 shows forth his attitude in face of the established powers, the emperor and his agents. There is here a diplomatic approach toward regaining the imperial circles for the orthodox cause. No matter what the circumstances were, Basil saw in the basileus *the representative of God on earth and the "friend of the Logos," in charge of maintaining the right order in Christendom. But at the same time, Basil never omitted to remind the imperial officials of the canonical prerogatives of the episcopate and the duty of bishops to exclude from their communion those who were deemed unworthy. We open the series with the following letter of Basil to Demosthenes.*

143

BASIL TO DEMOSTHENES, LETTER 225 (375)

We have always been grateful to God and to the emperors who care for us, when we see the government of our country entrusted to a man who is first a Christian and also a righteous man, exact guardian of the laws that govern our human destiny. It is especially when you arrived that we offered our prayers of thanksgiving to God, for our *basileus* "beloved of God" [θεοφιλεῖ]. Realizing that some enemies of the peace prepared to disturb the decisions of your venerable court concerning us, we did wait to be called by Your Magnanimity, in order that you be informed of the truth, insofar as you would claim, in your superior wisdom, the prerogative of examining ecclesiastical affairs. But the tribunal has by-passed us, and your authority, deceived as it was by the calumnies of Philocharis, ordered the arrest of our brother and concelebrant Gregory, who submitted to the decision—for how could he do otherwise? . . . If the problem to be examined is one of canonical order, and if Your Magnanimity claims for himself the right to hear the argument and pronounce the judgment, the presence of all of us [bishops] is necessary, for if there has been any canonical defect, the consecrators of the accused one [Gregory] are responsible, not he who has been obliged to accept the sacred office. Therefore we beseech you to leave to us the hearing of the argument in this country, not to have it transferred to a foreign land, nor to oblige us to meet with bishops with whom we have not yet reached an agreement concerning ecclesiastical procedure.

The deportation of Gregory of Nyssa was not unexpected. A synod of Arian bishops meeting at Tyana had inspired it. Gregory appears to have expressed his apprehension to Gregory of Nazianzus, who answered with rather cheap,

reassuring notes: "A storm indeed! The best is to let it pass!"
(Letters 72 and 74).

GREGORY OF NAZIANZUS TO GREGORY OF NYSSA:
LETTER 72 (375)

Do not fear too much the bite of affliction. If we feel
less afflicted, it is because it should affect us less. It is not
amazing that the heretics would have warmed themselves
up and, now that spring is coming, dare to crawl out of their
holes, as you write. They will hiss a little, I know, then they
will burrow again under the pressure of truth and time, all
the more if we put everything in God's hand.

GREGORY OF NAZIANZUS TO GREGORY OF NYSSA:
LETTER 74 (375)

While staying here, I accompany you in love, for affection makes everything common between us. And I have
good hope, trusting in God's love for men and in your
prayers, that all things will turn out according to your desire,
that the tempest will abate into a soft breeze, and that the
God of orthodoxy will give you, as a reward, to prevail
against the calumniators. Above all, may we see you back
soon and meet with you again, as we wish! But if you are
delayed, should circumstances so determine, do not refuse
to inform us by letters of your actual condition, and pray for
us, as you used to do. May the good God grant you health
and prosperity in all things, you who art the common support
of the Church!

These letters of Gregory of Nazianzus had been over-optimistic. Basil was less confident. It was obvious that Demosthenes aimed at eliminating the partisans of the archbishop of Caesaraea from the eparchy of the south, and Basil wrote (Letter 237) to a fellow bishop, Eusebius of Samosata, how he felt about Demosthenes' machinations. A couple of years later, Eusebius himself would be exiled by order of Demosthenes (Basil's letter 268).

BASIL TO EUSEBIUS, BISHOP OF SAMOSATA (SYRIA), LETTER 237 (376)

. . . An imperial vicar [βικάριος, viz. Demosthenes] has arrived here; it was the first and greatest of our calamities! Whether the man has heretical feelings I do not know. It seems to me that he is totally ignorant of the doctrine, and has no zeal whatever or interest about such problems; I see him utterly concerned, soul and body, day and night, with other things. Anyway, he is the friend of heretics and has as much love for them as hatred for us. He has gathered a synod of lawless people in Galatia in the midst of winter. . . . He has ordered my brother Gregory to be arrested as guilty, by a man—a low-class fellow at that—and after busying himself with some army matters for a short time, he came back to us, breathing anger and violence, and with one single word he delivered to the senate [the βουλή] all the clerics of the Church at Caesaraea.

Here follows a series of letters addressed by Basil to Orthodox bishops who had been deported by order of Valens. The persecution had not been restricted to the sole provinces of Anatolia, but had spread to Syria and to Egypt, where the imperial administration had to deal with populations of a different ethnic background, Syrians and Copts superficially Hellenized, but intent upon retaining their rites and customs, together with the Nicene bishops to whom Basil is now writing.

BASIL TO BARSAS, BISHOP OF EDESSA (URFA), WHO WAS IN EXILE, LETTER 264 (ca. 377)

To Barsas, truly beloved of God, bishop worthy of all respect and esteem, from Basil, greetings in the Lord! Since the trusted brothers of Domninos are going to Your Piety, we welcome with joy the occasion of sending you these letters and greeting you through these brethren. We pray Holy God to keep us still in this life until we are deemed worthy to see you and to enjoy the gifts [χαρίσματα] which are in you. Only pray that the Lord not deliver us forever to enemies of the cross of Christ, but guard his Churches until the day of peace; this peace the Just Judge knows when he will give back. But as he had fixed a duration of seventy years of exile to the Israelites for their sins, perhaps the Almighty, after handing us over to our enemies for a term, will remember us and re-establish us in the peace that was at the origin, unless the great apostasy be near and the actual events be the prelude of the coming of the Antichrist. If this is it, pray that the good God avert the calamity from us or help us pass through it without stumbling. We greet through you all the worthy company that surrounds Your Piety. All who are with us greet Your Piety. Be well and rejoice in the Lord, pray for me, and may you be conserved to the Church of God, by the Grace of the Holy One!

Basil to Eulogios, Alexander and Adelphokration, Egyptian bishops in exile, Letter 265 (377)

We discover in all things how great is the providence of the good God toward his Churches. Some events are ominous and seem to happen without a purpose, but even fortuitous events are ordained to the utility of the greater number, in the wisdom of God and His justice, which cannot possibly be traced. See this: the Lord has raised up your love from the regions of Egypt to bring it into the heart of Palestine and establish it, as was typified by Israel of old, whom he exiled into the land of the Assyrians in order to extinguish their idolatry at the advent of the saints. Now we have found by reflection that the Lord, in placing this ordeal before you, has opened unto you, through exile, the stadium of blessed contests, and has bestowed upon those who happen to meet you the gift of a clear model of the principles leading to salvation. We have learned, through the grace of God, the correctness of your faith, your solicitude for the brethren, and that you do not negligently by-pass things of common interest or which are necessary for salvation, but give precedence to whatever promotes the edification of the Churches. So we have sent the beloved Elpidios, our fellow servant of God [συνδιάκονον], to carry this letter to you and, as much as he is capable, to inform you of what we may have overlooked in our letter. What has most encouraged us in our desire of fellowship with you is the report of your pious zeal for the right doctrine; neither the countless libels nor the variety of sophisms have shaken the steadfastness of your heart. You have denounced those who innovate in matters of apostolic dogma; you have not accepted to remain silent on the harm they do. We found that all who cleave to the peace of the Lord were greatly afflicted by the manifold novelties of Apollinaris of Laodicaea. . . . His discourses on God, do they not abound in impious teachings and in the older impiety of that fool Sabellius, reviving it in recent treatises? . . . Renewing past errors, Apollinaris announces now the restoration of the Temple, the minute observance of the legal ritual, the figurative High Priest after the true High Priest [cf. Heb 7:15-17], the guilt-offerings [1 Sm 6:3, Lv 14-19] after the Lamb of God has taken away the sins of the world [Jn 1:29], partial baptisms [βαπτίσματα μερικά: anabaptism?], after the *one* baptism [Eph 4:5], the ashes of a heifer [Nb 19:1-10] to sprinkle the Church which through faith in Christ has neither spot nor wrinkle nor any such blemish [Eph 5:27], the rite of purification of lepers [Lv 14:2], after the imperviousness to injury after the Resurrection, the offering of jealousy [προσφορὰ ζηλο-τυπίας, Nb 5:14-15], when humans shall neither wed nor be wed [viz. in the resurrection, Mt 23:30], the showbreads [ἄρτοι προθέσεως, Ex 25:30], after the bread from heaven [Jn 6:32], lighted lamps, after Him who is the True Light [Jn 1:19]! After all, if the precepts of the Law have been abrogated by our dogmas, then it is clear that the dogmas of Christ would be nullified if the precepts of the Law were restored!

BASIL TO EUSEBIUS, BISHOP OF SAMOSATA,
IN EXILE, LETTER 268 (378)

The Lord has shown that even in our time He would not abandon His saints and that His great and mighty hand would protect the life of Your Sanctity. Your case is nearly like the case of the holy man who remained unharmed in the belly of a whale, or of the God-fearing men who remained alive in a furious fire [Jon 1:17; Dn 3]. Whereas war, as I hear, surrounds you on all parts, the Lord has preserved Your Piety safe and sound, so let Almighty God keep watch over you—a prospect most desirable for us if we are still alive, or at any rate, for others who await your return as if it were their own salvation. I am confident that the God who loves men [ὁ φιλάνθρωπος], heedful of the tears of the Churches and of the moaning of all who moan for you, shall keep you in this life, until he grants the petitions of those who pray to him night and day. What was done among you until the arrival of our dear brother Libanios, our fellow minister [συνδιακόνου], we heard from him well enough when he passed by our place, but we are eager to know what has happened since, for we have heard that in the meantime many worse calamities have occurred over there. May we hear from you as soon as possible, or at least through our pious brother and fellow priest Paul [συνπρε-σβυτέρου] when he returns; and may your life remain safely and soundly preserved, as we wish! Because we have learned that all the roads are full of gangsters and deserters, we dared not entrust anything in the hands of this brother, for fear we might be the involuntary cause of his being murdered. If the Lord grants us a measure of respite, we shall hurry to send you one of our people to visit with you and report unto us whatever happened in your region.

Gregory of Nazianzus, prevented from taking possession of his Church of Sasima in the southwestern eparchy of Cappadocia, and unwilling, after the death of his father, to occupy the throne of Nazianzus otherwise than as a temporary caretaker, received a call to the Orthodox community of Constantinople. The congregation was overwhelmingly outnumbered by pagans, sectarians of every description, and the Arians who had the favor of Emperor Valens. His police could keep an eye on the tiny church—we might say a "house-church"—where the Orthodox gathered for the liturgical services; Gregory called it the "Anastasia." Valens was killed in a campaign against invaders from Scythia, or was mur-dered—anyway disappeared from the scene after 378. His successor Theodosius "the Great," devoted to the Nicene faith, was enthroned in the autumn of 380, but was not able to assert his authority immediately, or control the populace and restore an acceptable order. In a letter addressed to a certain Theodoros—not otherwise identified unless he is the bishop of Tyana—Gregory writes how, as he was officiating at the baptism of catechumens on Great and Holy Saturday, a mob of howling monks, shrieking females, and street hoodlums invaded the chapel and hurled stones at the congregation. The confirmation of Gregory on the patriarchal throne of Constantinople by the Council of 381 was bound to remain largely ineffectual as, sick at heart and weary, he decided to retire to his estate of Kerbela near Nazianzus.

GREGORY OF NAZIANZUS TO THEODOROS, LETTER 77
(written during Holy Week 379 or 380)

I hear that you have been dismayed by the news that we were assaulted by riotous monks and hoodlums. No wonder this appears to you intolerable; you have thus far escaped being beaten, and you been spared our ordeals. As for us, used to being mistreated and to having our share of outrage, we may be expected to address Your Piety with the exhortations that old age teaches and reason suggests. Yes, these events are atrocious, more than atrocious; who would contest this? They have desecrated the altars, profaned the mysteries. As we stood between those to be baptized and those who were throwing stones at us, we had no recourse against the stoning except prayer. Virgins have given up modesty, monks have renounced decency, street-beggars have forsaken their lowly station in life. Anger has deprived them of all pity. Yet, in what we suffer, it is better to be patient and give to many an example of longanimity. Words do not persuade a crowd, but acts do, being a silent exhortation. We believe strongly in punishing evildoers; strongly, I say, because it is useful for the correction of others, but it is

still better and more godly to endure stoically. Punishment
bridles wickedness; but firmness under misfortune persuades
people to be good, and this is much better than simply not
being wicked. Let us believe that a great occasion of clem-
ency [φιλανθρωπία] is offered to us, in order that we may
obtain to be forgiven, and let us add goodness to goodness!

*A sequel to the events described in letter 77: The ad-
dressee, a certain Theoteknos, his wife, and his daughter
were among the catechumens recently baptized by Gregory,
and victims of the ruffians who had disrupted the ceremony—
a sacrilege calling for the rigors of the Law! Gregory, writing
to Theoteknos, seizes the occasion for continuing his little
homily on the superior values of Christian forgiveness.*

GREGORY OF NAZIANZUS TO THEOTEKNOS, LETTER 78
(Shortly After Easter 379)

We know that it is difficult to accept reasoning when
injury is recent and when anger is still boiling. Anger and
grief are blind, especially when irritation is justified. However, since we have been among those who have been injured and violently abused, and since we are equally indig-
nant as you, we deserve for this not to be overlooked when
we give you advice. We have been awfully mistreated; add,
if you like, that no other man was mistreated as we have
been. But this should not be a reason for injuring ourselves
and being discouraged from devotion to our own detriment.
A wife is a great thing; a daughter a most precious good;
not more precious, however, than our soul. Consider that
yesterday you were made worthy of grace and that through

baptism you were purified of your sins; now there is a temptation which is not to be taken lightly: spoiling by a bloody vengeance the gift received and thus being in need of a second purification [possible allusion to a rite of sacramental penance]. Let us stop conspiring against ourselves, let us not reject our trust in God by a display of violence and of immoderate indignation against those who have mistreated us. The man [whom Theoteknos wanted to bring before the Law], let us deliver him to God and to yonder chastisement. As for us, we should render the Judge indulgent toward us by showing ourselves indulgent and, by forgiving, be forgiven. Let not some captious reasoning deceive you. Someone may have legitimate reasons for calling another man to justice, and then he is without reproach. So also is one who delivers a law-breaker to the Law. There are the laws of Rome, but there are also our Christian laws. The former are inflexible, harsh, and bloody. Our laws are useful, humane, and they do not let us abuse angrily the guilty party. We ought to abide by the latter and observe them, so that by doing small favors—and since life is short and of no value—we may receive from God big favors, His love, and our hope for the beyond.

Meantime Gregory of Nyssa, once the general situation in Cappadocia permitted it, was able to retake possession of his bishopric, from which he had been evicted and exiled under Valens. In letter 6 he describes to bishop Ablabios his triumphal return to his episcopal town. Thunder and rainstorms raged during his journey—autumnal equinox?— described with gusto and a point of humor. The date is to be sought toward the time of the first Council of Constantinople (381).

GREGORY OF NYSSA TO BISHOP ABLABIOS, LETTER 6

The Lord has saved us, most likely on account of the prayers that you offered for us, and I shall relate to you this evident proof of God's kindness. We had already left behind us the region of Kelousa when there came suddenly a mass of clouds, and the clear sky turned into a thick darkness. A cold breeze, moist and wet, blowing from the clouds around our bodies, threatened to burst out into a rainstorm. On our left, continuous thundering tore through the sky, and flashes of lightning followed one another before each thunderclap. The mountains ahead of us and behind us, on the right and on the left, were hidden by the clouds. But now the large cloud hanging over our head was chased sideways by a violent tempest, and we ourselves, like it happened miraculously to the Israelites [Ex 14:22], being surrounded on all sides by water, passed on dry foot to Ouestena [unidentified]. Thoroughly tired, we took some rest with our mules. We were given by God signs of rainy weather ahead. After three or four hours of sufficient rest in that place, God divided once more the clouds of rain, and the chariot moved more easily on the surface of beaten clay, on which the wheels turned freely. Now the road from this place to our town winds along the river, which is serving the entire region downstream. Small settlements, not much distant from one another, line the road, and this continuous suite of villages was full of people, who came to meet us and escort us, all of them showing forth a mixture of joy and tears. A light drizzle moistened the air. A little before our town, a cloud above our heads burst into a shower of rain, and this enabled us to proceed quite unnoticed. At the entrance gate of the colonnade [the στοά], aroused by the noise of the chariot on the hard pavement, a crowd of people, as driven by a secret force, closed on us round about, so that we could not even descend from the carriage, for no empty space could be found. The people could hardly be persuaded to allow us to descend and let the mules go on. These excessive demonstrations of love and joy brought us to the point of fainting. Having advanced a little in the colonnade and approaching the door of the church, we saw something like a river of fire streaming into the church. It was the choirs of the virgins, holding wax-tapers, facing one another and singing at the entrance of the church, which was illumined by ardent torches. We entered the church, rejoicing and weeping with the people, who were affected as much as we ourselves, and the crowd being moved from joy to tears. I ordered the praying to be ended, and forthwith wrote this letter to Your Holiness, after which I paused to quench my thirst, and attended to my bodily needs!

9
Hierarchs' Frustrations

Hierarchs are not continually "defining the word of truth" or leading the fight against heretics, but they cannot avoid being continually besieged by petitioners and claimants who expect the bishop to solve their personal problems, whether about serious matters or trifles, at times ludicrous. To these unwelcome distractions from the hierarchs' main task add the case of insubordinate clergy who take it upon themselves to act in their administration without much regard for canonical procedure: the canons are for specialists, and the bishop lives far away and is not always accessible!

Several letters from Basil deal with abuses committed, more or less innocently, by "village bishops," the "chorepiscopi" (χωρεπίσκοποι). These were church leaders invested with quasi-episcopal authority, under the jurisdiction of the bishop and the metropolitan of the ecclesiastical province. They were commonly addressed as episcopi, *without restrictive qualification. It appears from Basil's letters 53 and 54 that some of these* chorepiscopi *indulged in practices smacking of simony and ordained some unworthy candidates, in violation of regular canonical procedure.*

BASIL TO THE "VILLAGE BISHOPS" (χωρεπίσκοποι),
LETTER 53 (written at the beginning of his
episcopacy, 370-371)

The sordid affair about which I am writing, source of all kinds of mistrust and gossip, has filled my soul with grief, and to this day it sounds to me unbelievable. What I write a man who is conscious of guilt should take as a remedy, a conscientious man as preventive, and the indifferents—I pray that not many be found among you—as a solemn protest. But what am I talking about? It has been reported that some among you receive money from candidates for ordination, under pretense of piety, which is worse; for he who does something under pretense of the good deserves a double punishment, because he does that which is bad in itself, and he uses the good, so to speak, as an accomplice. If that is the case, let no one do this any more, but correct himself, for we must say to those who receive the silver what the Apostles said to the one who wanted to give some money for buying a share of the Holy Spirit: "Thy silver perish with thee!" [Ac 8:20]. Lesser indeed is the sin of him who, through ignorance, wanted to buy God's gift than the sin of him who puts it for sale; for there has in fact been a sale, and that which you have freely received, if you sell it, you shall be stripped of God's grace as if you had sold yourself to Satan, whenever you introduce that shabby trade of yours into things spiritual and into the Church, where the body and the blood of Christ are entrusted to us. This ought not to be! I am going to tell you what the stratagem is about: those sinners do not think they are sinning because they have not received the money *before,* but *after* the ordination [of the candidates]. Now, whether they have received it afterwards or in advance, receiving is receiving anyway. Give up, therefore, this sordid income; it is rather a passport to Hell. Do not soil your hands with such gains which make you unworthy to handle the holy mysteries.

BASIL TO "VILLAGE BISHOPS," LETTER 54,
(written at the beginning of his episcopacy, 370-371)

I am most saddened by the fact that the canons of the Fathers are henceforth forsaken, and that their strict observance is driven out of the Churches. I am afraid to see indifference progressing little by little and the affairs of the Church becoming utterly confused. Clerics, according to a policy that had existed from early times in the Church of God, used to be received after a most exacting examination; the course of their life was scrutinized to ascertain that they were not rowdies, or winebibbers, or violent, but that they kept their vehemence in check and were able to reach that holiness "without which no one shall see the Lord" [Heb 12:14]. The priests and deacons with whom they were living conducted the inquiry and made their report to the bishop in order that the candidates be inscribed on the roll of candidates to sacred orders [τῷ τάγματι τῶν ἱερατικῶν]. But now you have done away with this procedure and you have not even deigned to report to us. By so doing, you have appropriated the entire authority to yourselves. Through negligence in this case you have permitted the priests and the deacons to act from motives of kinship or friendship, and to introduce into the Church unworthy ministers as they pleased, without examining their life. For these reasons, one counts numerous clerics in every borough, and yet not one of them worthy of serving at the altar, as you witness yourselves, faced with a penury of suitable candidates. I see, therefore, that the entire situation has become irremediable, especially now that a great many are being inducted into the Church just to escape the military conscription. So I have decided to renew the canons of the Fathers; I order you to send me the list of all the clerics in every borough and to let me know by whom they were received and what their manner of life is. Cleanse the Church from the unworthy ones and from now on examine and receive only those who prove worthy, but do not enlist them before you report to us, or know that he shall be held a layman [λαϊκός, derogatively] who will have been received into the ministry without my approval.

Basil's letters 58, 59, and 60, written from Caesaraea, could be titled "A Family Affair." Basil's old uncle, Gregory, a Cappadocian chorepiscopos, had been censured by his nephew the metropolitan for some infractions of church discipline, like soliciting gifts of money for the administration of sacraments, an irregular but unfortunately widespread practice at the time. Now Basil's younger brother Gregory, the future bishop of Nyssa, feeling sorry for the old man, imagined to send to brother Basil a letter allegedly written by the uncle to apologize and beg for pardon—a neat case of forgery! But Basil discovered the fraud, and Gregory junior did not invent any better remedy to the imbroglio than forging two more letters! Basil, as could be expected, rebuked his brother and his uncle in no uncertain terms. The tone of letter 60, once Basil had affirmed his superior authority, softens considerably, and Basil continues to show a sincere reverence to the old churchman. As for brother Gregory, even after his elevation to the see of Nyssa, he remains for Basil the "little brother" and the prankster, well-meaning, but never quite to be trusted.

BASIL TO GREGORY OF NYSSA, LETTER 58 (371)

How should I dispute with you by letter? How should I scold you for your naïveté about everything? Who, do tell me, falls three times into the same nets? Who is caught three times in the same trap? That would not happen to a beast!

You brought a letter which you had concocted as if it were from the venerable bishop our common uncle. I do not know why you want to cheat me. I received that letter, believing it was a letter by the bishop. Could I do anything else but accept it? I have shown it to many friends, from the joy I had, giving grace to God. But the forgery was discovered, when the bishop himself [Chorepiscopos Gregory] denied having ever written that letter. It made us utterly ashamed; we prayed that the earth would split open, as we were all disgraced and enmeshed in lying and deceit. Then another letter was delivered to me, allegedly sent by the bishop himself and carried by your servant Asterios. Neither was this second letter authentic, as the bishop testified before our venerable brother Anthimos, who notified us. And there was a third letter, which Adamantios brought to us. How were we to receive what was sent to us by you and your people? I wished I had a heart of stone, so that I would neither remember the past nor be ashamed of the present, so that I could bear the strokes, my head low, like the beasts! But how act reasonably after a first and a second experience, unless I were able to accept anything without inquiry? I am writing this to upbraid you for your simplicity—simplicity indeed behooves a Christian—but I do not see how it fits in this particular instance. At any rate, be on your guard for the future and spare me, for I must tell you frankly that in such things you are not a trustworthy servant! No matter who were the messengers, we have replied appropriately. Now, if it were to vex me further, or because you had received the letter you sent me really from the bishop, here is the answer. It is likely that you have other concerns for the moment. You are my brother, you have not yet forgotten nature, and you do not regard us as taking part with the enemy. We have entered a way of life which grinds down our body and wears out our soul beyond our own strength. All the same, since you started the war, you should take your stand and act accordingly. It is said: "brothers must help in necessity" [cf. Sirach 40:24]. If the venerable bishops do agree to a meeting with us, let them designate a precise place and time and send their own people to fetch us. I am

not reluctant to go and meet my uncle, but if it is not done
in the proper form, I shall not accept it.

BASIL TO HIS UNCLE GREGORY, LETTER 59 (371)

"I kept silent. Shall I always be silent?" [cf. Is 42:14].
Have I to bear longer the unbearable pain of silence and not
write? Shall I not hear anyone talking to me? Having per-
severed thus far in this gloomy disposition, I suppose it is
appropriate now to say with the prophet: "I have endured
pain like the woman in childbirth" [Is 42:14]. I have always
desired an accord by word of mouth, and always I failed
because of my sinfulness. I could imagine no other cause
for the present situation, were it not my conviction that I
am paying the price for my old sins by being estranged from
your love. And when I speak of estrangement, I do not mean
being a stranger to the first passer-by, but our being mutually
estranged from each other, whereas you have been to me as a
father since the earliest time. But now my sinfulness, holding
me as under a dense cloud, has made me unaware of all
those things. If I consider that besides the pain to endure
what is happening no happy issue can be expected to this
whole affair, have I not a reason for imputing the present
situation to my own wickedness? If it is my sin that is the
cause of whatever has happened, let it be the end of our
troubles; if it is the result of some machination, the intended
result was fully realized. This is why, being unable to contain
myself, I have first raised my voice, begging you to remember me, and to remember yourself as well, for you have
shown during all your life a greater protection to me than
the protection of mere kinship demands. And now, do love
our city [Caesaraea] for our sake, rather than bearing it a
grudge because of us. If there is some consolation in Christ,
if there is some communion of the Spirit, if there are some

feelings of mercy, do fulfill our wish: put a stop at once to all that disgrace, prepare the beginning of a brighter future by being yourself a guide to others into what is best, lest they follow a road they should not take. Till now, no mark has been recognized in anyone which would distinguish him as clearly as the peaceful and conciliatory dispositions of your own soul. It is fitting therefore that with those qualities you would draw the others to you and let all who approach you be filled with the excellence of your *mores* as if it were a fragrance of myrrh. And if there is some resistance now, after a short time it will be acknowledged how good peace itself is. But as long as slanders and calumnies take place, suspicion shall necessarily increase and always become worse. To be sure it is wrong for hostile people to slight us, and it is still more wrong that they should slight Your Reverence. If we have sinned in any way, we will amend ourselves, once we have been admonished. But this cannot be done, short of our coming together. If we have not done anything wrong, why are we hated? Here is what I may advance for my own justification.

What the Churches say on their behalf—they draw no great benefit from our divisions!—it is better not to mention it. To bring affliction to anyone is not my idea, but rather to avoid affliction. You will discover it yourself and tell others much better and more fully than I can figure out, for you saw before we did the damages inflicted upon the Churches, and you are afflicted more than we, since you have been taught for a long time by the Lord not to despise the smallest things. Now the damage is not limited to one or two persons among us, but entire cities and regions bear with us the same miseries. Must we then publish abroad what is being said about us? It would be fitting for Your Magnanimity to leave quarrelsomeness to others, even more, to uproot it from their soul if possible, and for you to overcome grievances through resignation. Vengeance belongs to anyone in anger, but to dominate anger itself belongs only to you and to those who come close to you in virtue. What I will not say is that if someone is angry at us, he unleashes his anger against some who have done no wrong. Therefore, whether by your presence or by letters, by an invitation to meet with you, or in whatever way you choose, do comfort our soul. Our wish is that your piety shine upon the Church and that you bring relief unto us and unto the people as well, if only we may see you or hear your gracious words. If that is possible, it will be best; but if you prefer another way, we will agree to it. Only let us know your suggestions, that your wisdom may be of help.

BASIL TO HIS UNCLE GREGORY, LETTER 60 (371)

Till now I saw my brother [Gregory of Nyssa] with pleasure. How could it be otherwise since he is my brother, and what a brother! It was in this very same disposition that I did welcome him on his arrival, my affection for him being unchanged. Let nothing make me forget nature or contend against my kinsmen. Amidst my bodily ailments and the other grievances of my soul, I regarded the presence of your man [a messenger] as an encouragement, and the letters he brought from Your Reverence did relieve me still more. For a long time I desired to receive them, for the sole reason that I refused to add to the gloom by describing a quarrel between close relatives; it would give pleasure to our enemies, sadden our friends, and offend God, who has impressed the character of perfect love on his own disciples. That is why I must answer and beg you to pray for us and otherwise care for me as kinsman. Regarding what actually happened, since I do not understand it in my stupidity, I have decided to hold as true the explanation you will deign to give me. But it is necessary that the rest also be settled by Your Magnanimity, namely our meeting together at an appropriate time and a convenient place; therefore, if Your Reverence accepts to lower himself to our humility and give us some word, either with other people or, if you prefer, in a private interview, we shall agree. Once and for all we have resolved to serve you in love and to do whatever Your Grace shall write us, for the glory of God. As for our venerable brother [Gregory of Nyssa], we did not want to oblige him to say anything orally, because thus far his word has not been confirmed by his works.

A group of three letters relative to the misbehavior of a certain Glykerios, a deacon of the church of Venasa near Nazianzus, has been attributed by the Maurist editors to Basil, reproduced in Courtonne's French translation (Budé collection), and numbered 169, 170, and 171. They are more likely to have been written by Gregory of Nazianzus while he was the acting caretaker of the Church of his father. See A. Cavallin, Studien zu den Briefen des Hl. Basilius, Lund, 1944, *pp. 81-92, quoted in the French edition of Gregory of Nazianzus' letters, II., p. 170, and numbered 246, 247, and 248. We follow the Greek text of Gallay, letters 246, 247, and 248 of Gregory of Nazianzus.*

GREGORY OF NAZIANZUS TO BASIL, LETTER 246
(written after 372)

A fine task of indulgence and philanthropy you have undertaken, gathering together the captives of "brazen-faced" Glykerios—for the moment, that's how we'll describe him—and trying to cover, if possible, our common shame! All the same, Your Discretion must learn of his case and put an end to the scandal. This swaggering Glykerios who imposes upon you, we had ordained him a deacon by the "laying of hands" [χειροτονία] to the local church of Venasa [Οὐήνασα], for serving the priest and supervising the work in that church. And indeed the man, though he be of a rather difficult character, nonetheless shows some aptitude for this sort of work. Once appointed, he did as if he had never been assigned to this task. He gathered some wretched girls on his own authority and initiative; some of them flocked toward him—you know how young folks are inclined to do such things—and others he constrained and undertook to guide, assuming the title and attire of an abbot [σχῆμα πατρι-αρχίας]. And he began strutting about without any right motive of piety. He aimed at nothing else but a means of living such as people would find any other way, and he nearly turned the entire Church upside down: despising his priest, a man venerable by his character and his age, despising the *chorepiscopos* and ourself as negligible, filling up the town and the entire clergy with confusion and trouble. Finally, having been admonished by us and by the *chorepiscopos* to be less arrogant—he had even trained young men [ἐγύμναζεν] unto the same folly—he conceived a wild and adventurous enterprise: kidnapping all the girls he could, he waited for the night and ran away with the fugitives. This may seem to you awful enough, but consider the time: we were celebrating the local feast and naturally people flocked together from everywhere. So Glykerios brought along his "corps de ballet," leading all those youngsters to dance around, to the great scandal of pious persons and the great glee of libertines or people always ready for gossip. But, serious as it is, this is not all. As I hear, the parents of the girls, who refused to be deprived of their children and tried to bring that "dispersion" back home, wailing and throwing themselves at the feet of their daughters, as we may well imagine—that amazing young fellow insulted and abused them, along with his gang of pirates. Let not these things appear tolerable to Your Piety, for the mockery affects us all. First of all, command him to return with the girls. He might be shown some indulgence if he comes back with a letter of yours. If not, do at least turn the girls back to their mother, the Church. But if you cannot, do not allow those willing to yield to continue being tyrannized in that manner.

Persuade them to return to us, or we shall call God and men to witness that such a situation is wrong and contrary to the right order of the Church. As for Glykerios, if he presents himself sobered and having recovered a correct attitude, so much the better! But if not, let him know that he is deposed from his office.

GREGORY OF NAZIANZUS TO GLYKERIOS, LETTER 247

Till when shall you rave and persist in your evil counsel, provoking us and dishonoring the entire order of monks? Turn back to God and to us confidently, for we wish to follow the example of His "philanthropy." We have rebuked you in a fatherly way; we shall also pardon you as a father: this is what we want to tell you. Many implore us on your behalf; your own priest, whose age and compassion we respect, more than any others. But if you continue to stray from us, know that you have fallen from your rank and have parted with God, since your songs and your robe drive the girls not to God, but to the abyss.

GREGORY OF NAZIANZUS TO BASIL, LETTER 248

I wrote to you not long ago about Glykerios and the girls. They have not yet returned, up to this day. Why or how I do not know. I am not going to accuse you of managing this case in a way that would expose us to criticism, whether you bear us some grudge, or in order to please others. Let them [Glykerios and the girls] come back without fear; do vouch for this! It pains us to see these members cut off from the Churches, even though they would be rightly cut off. But if they persist, let the burden of it be carried by them. We wash our hands of it.

A long letter, atrributed to Gregory of Nazianzus (No. 249), or to Gregory of Nyssa (No. 1), gives a vivid description of the mishaps of one of our hierarchs in the inhospitable region of Greater Armenia and his unplanned meeting with Helladios, successor of St Basil on the metropolitan see of Caesaraea. Helladios happened to be traveling in the same region and proved to be no more comfortable than the craggy district. The presumed date of the letter is the period between 379 and 382-383, when the province of Cappadocia, divided under Valens into Cappadocia Prima and Cappadocia Secunda, was tentatively reunified under Theodosius for a short time. (See the critical discussion in Gallay and Pasquali). The attribution to Gregory of Nazianzus rather than to Gregory of Nyssa seems the most probable. The identification of Flavianos, the addressee, is uncertain. He is likely to have been Flavianos of Antioch, a partisan of the Eastern bishops during the so-called "schism of Meletios," over against the party of Paulinus, favored by the Westerners and Pope Damascus. As for Helladios, who appears in the letter to Flavianos as a boor without manners, his relations with Gregory of Nazianzus had at first been friendly: notes of Paschal greetings, letters of Gregory recommending his nephews the elder Nikoboulos and Nikoboulos, Jr., the latter being in his charge as praefectus mansionis, *"master of communications," a kind of regional postmaster at the much frequented thermal springs of Xanxaris near Tyana in the second Cappadocia. But Gregory of Nazianzus had turned sour (letters 219 and 220) when he reproached the metropolitan for failing to support the old priest Sakerdos against calumniators. The letter to Flavianos mentions a certain Peter who had died recently, and whose anniversary was to be celebrated by Helladios together with the liturgies in honor of the forty martyrs of Sebastaea. G. Pasquali esteems that this Peter is probably different from the youngest brother of Basil and Gregory of Nyssa; the latter would not have missed identifying this "blessed Peter" as his own brother. This again makes it unlikely that the letter to Flavianos should be atributed to Gregory of Nyssa, and confirms the thesis in favor of Gregory of Nazianzus as the author of the letter.*

GREGORY OF NAZIANZUS, LETTER 249, OR
GREGORY OF NYSSA, LETTER 1, TO BISHOP FLAVIANOS
(379-382/3?)

Our predicament, O man of God, is not good! The bad dispositions of those who raise against us a hatred unjust and unjustified are no mere affair of supposition or suspicion, but come out in the open as if they were a right move for the good. . . . Some people have insinuated that the Most Reverend Helladios showed some hostility toward us and told everyone that I was for him the cause of the worst troubles. I did not believe these gossips, examining my conscience and the actual facts. Yet the same things were reported to us from all sides in the same terms as if to confirm the rumor, and I realized that one should not engage lightly in a conflict which had neither root nor substance. So I wrote immediately to Your Grace and advised other influential persons to become involved. Finally, after passing some time with the Sebastenes [inhabitants of Sebastaea], who celebrated for the first time the memory of the most blessed Peter and, on the same occasion, commemorated the holy martyrs, I started back to return to my Church. I was told at that time that Helladios was in the mountainous region nearby, celebrating the memory of the martyrs. At first I

continued on my way, judging that it was more appropriate
to meet with him in the metropolis, but one of my people
came by and informed me that Helladios was sick. Having
heard this, I left my carriage and decided to visit him,
traveling on horseback along precipitous and nigh-impassa-
ble mountain paths. The distance, according to the local
people, was fifteen mile stones. I negotiated that distance with
great pains, partly walking, partly riding; on the morrow,
after having traveled part of the night, I arrived at daybreak
at Andaèmon [a locality in Armenia]—that is the name of
the borough where Helladios sat in assembly with two other
bishops. From afar, standing on a hill above the place, we
saw the assembly sitting in the open air outside the church
and we approached slowly, my companions and I, dismount-
ing and leading the horses by the bridle, just as Helladios was
leaving to return to his lodgings, at which time we arrived
at the *martyrion*. Without delay we sent someone to inform
him of our presence. After a few minutes, the deacon at-
tached to his service appeared and we urged him to inform
the bishop, so that we might converse with him at some
length, as we were desirous to find an occasion of clearing
the difference that alienated us. Hereupon I remained, sitting in the open air and expecting that somebody would
invite me in; there I was, exposed as an odd spectacle to the
people who came for the feast. . . . After much ado the
doors were opened unto us and we entered into Helladios'
apartment, but no one of our party was admitted inside
except my deacon, who sustained with his arm my exhausted
body. I saluted Helladios and remained standing for a while,
expecting he would offer me a seat, but he did not. So I
turned around toward a bench which was there, and rested,
waiting for him to address us with some polite word, or
give us a sign from his eyebrows, but all our hope was deceived. . . . My mind was stupefied at all this. He would not
even gratify me with some conversational phrases like "Are
you all right?" or "How did you come?" "What for?" "Did
it just happen or was it for some business?" "Were you so
eager to come here?" . . . Then I said to Helladios: "Perhaps
my presence interferes with some medical treatment pre-

scribed for your health. Should I rather leave you now?" He answered gruffly that he needed no assistance and I said a few words to quiet him down, if possible. But he declared that he had some grievances against us on account of many offenses. . . . I replied: "My conscience is perfectly clear in the matters that concern you. I hope to be forgiven for other sins of mine, but I have never wronged you and so I do not need ever to be forgiven for any sin against you." There he got angry and did not let me bring forth the proofs for my assertions. . . . It was past the sixth hour of the day [past twelve noon]. The bath was ready. The meal was being prepared. It was a Saturday and the feast of the martyrs. . . . After the exhaustion of our journey, parched by the burning heat which we had suffered while sitting in the open before Helladios' door, after the dismal sadness which affected us while we bore his glance, he dismissed us for the return journey by the same way we had come, weary and weakened to exhaustion. With great pain we caught up with our company, having suffered in the meantime a serious ordeal: a windstorm, followed by an ominous thundercloud and a violent rain shower. We were drenched to the bones, for, seeing the extreme heat, we had taken no precaution against rainy weather. Anyhow, through God's grace and after a good night's rest with our companions, we made it—alive—to our regions.

Relations with Armenians and Armenian Churches had always been a serious problem for bishops of Hellenic descent. Our three hierarchs had aimed at maintaining a friendly cooperation with the Armenian element, often unsuccessfully. They had to deal with a population Christianized of old, who saw no reason why they should relish the attitude of most bishops of Hellenic descent for whom the name "Christian" was synonymous with "Hellene." They tended to ignore the condition created by the plurality of populations under imperial rule. Gregory of Nazianzus' la-

conic letter 62 shows an undisguised impatience with an Armenian, to whom Amphilochios, who had not yet been consecrated bishop of Iconium, had shown some kindness.

GREGORY OF NAZIANZUS TO AMPHILOCHIOS, LETTER 62 (373)

The ruling of your inimitable kindness is not barbarous, but Greek and also Christian. As for that Armenian of whom you are so proud, he is obviously a barbarian, and he is far from doing us credit.

After resigning his see of Constantinople, Nazianzus retired to his estate of Kerbela, close to a chapel dedicated to the Martyrs, in the hope of finding some peace. His letter 203 is addressed to a certain Valentinianos—no friend of his— who has installed obstreperous females in a house nearby. Gregory protests against this juicy breach of neighborliness.

GREGORY OF NAZIANZUS TO VALENTINIANOS, LETTER 203

We have been expelled from Kerbela in "the most impious way" [ἀνοσιώτατα]—I am quoting from Euripides' tragedy [Phoenicians]. We were expelled not verbally [ἔργῳ], but factually [λόγῳ] and most violently. It would have been much easier to serve us notice to quit than to install opposite us a band of harpies who ruin the dignity of our life by subjecting us to daily disgrace and insults on the part of people bent upon decrying those who have chosen, like us, a different way of life. . . . You [Valentinianos], when you come into our region, will be received and welcomed, but we recoil from the comments of such females as if we were attacked by vipers. . . . As for you, may you inhabit this place longer than your predecessors; more wisely, we hope, so as not to offend the Holy Martyrs, and without being tortured for settling there. First of all, be careful; do not presume to lay hands on objects consecrated to the holy Martyrs! Otherwise the situation would turn badly for you and your property, and it would become even worse if you appropriated what is not yours.

10
Glimpses of Daily Life

The order in which we present our hierarchs' short notes, a considerable number of intimate messages well fit to inform us of their daily activities, is immaterial. We will arrange them in broad categories and will briefly comment on each piece, if need be.

Postal Service

Poorer still than ours! The imperial service, when available, could not be blindly trusted to respect the confidentiality of personal communications. Our hierarchs entrusted their letters to private messengers, often some deacon or a cleric in lesser orders, who would advise the addressee on what the author had deemed prudent not to put in writing, and would bring the answer back as soon as possible.

BASIL TO HIS FRIEND GREGORY OF NAZIANZUS, LETTER 19
(written before Basil's consecration to the episcopacy)

A letter addressed to me came lately from you. It was from you all right, judging from the handwriting, as well as from the proper object of the message; the words were few,

yet made much sense. I have not answered right away because we were absent, and the messenger, having delivered
the letter to one of our people, left and went away. Now I
write through Peter [Basil's younger brother], to send you
our due greetings, and also to give you an occasion for writing a second letter. No one ever tired from reading a laconic
letter, like the letters we receive from you every time.

*Basil had written several letters which failed to reach
Eusebius, who at that time was in Thrace, having some business with the imperial bureaucracy. Now that Eusebius was
back in his diocese, Basil describes his futile attempts to
reach him by mail in Thrace; the letter continues with a relation of the banishment of Gregory of Nyssa and the persecution of the Orthodox at the hand of the Arians (see chapter 8).*

BASIL TO EUSEBIUS OF SAMOSATA, LETTER 237 (376)

I had written to Your Piety a letter which the vicar
[βικάριος] of Thrace was supposed to bring to you; I had
also written other letters and asked the treasurer of Philip-
popolis who was going to return to Thrace to take these
letters on leaving from here. But the vicar was unable to take
your letters. As we were touring through our own diocese
[παροικία], this man [the vicar], who had arrived in town
in the evening, set out very early, and the people of the
church were not even aware of his passage; so the letters
remained here. As for the treasurer, hindered by some circumstances not of his choice, he started without taking the
letters and without having seen us. There was no way of finding another messenger, and we remained aggrieved that we
could neither write nor receive letters from Your Piety. Yet

I would have liked, had it been possible, to let you know what happened to us every day, for there were so many extraordinary things that it would take a journal. I would have written it, know it well, if the succession of events had not put off my plans for the future.

BASIL TO MELETIOS, BISHOP OF ANTIOCH IN SYRIA, LETTER 89 (372)

The good God, who procures us occasions to address Your Merit, appeases the excess of our yearning, for He is witness of our desire to contemplate your face and to enjoy your teaching, so good and profitable to the souls, right now, through the very pious and zealous brother, our fellow-servant at the altar [συνδιακόνου], who is leaving; we beg you to pray especially for us, that we be not a stumbling block to the people or hinder your prayers from moving the Lord. Furthermore we remind you to deign making arrangements for everything through the brother we have just mentioned, and, since we must write to the Westerners, because letters have to be carried by one of our people, to dictate those letters yourself. Having met Sabinos, the deacon they sent, we have written to the Illyrians, the bishops of Italy and Gaul, and to some of those who had written to us on their own. But it is advisable that someone be sent as from a common assembly and that he would carry a second letter, which you shall order to be written. With regard to the most venerable bishop Athanasius of Alexandria [295-373], we would remind you—your perfect wisdom understands this very well—that I cannot engage myself by letter or do anything useful if he does not accept your communion in some way, seeing that you declined to accept his own. He is said to be very amenable to unite with us and to cooperate as far as possible, but he deplores that he has been dismissed without being in communion [ἀκοινώνητος] and that so far he has received only vain promises. The present situation in Anatolia has certainly not escaped the ears of Your Piety and the brother we have mentioned shall report everything to you in greater detail. Kindly grant him his leave soon after Easter, because he expects the answers of those of Samosata. Welcome his zeal, comfort him by your prayers, and dispatch him to do what has been decided.

Basil writes to his fellow bishop of Samosata after several attempts of communicating by letters sent either through the imperial couriers or through private messengers. Letter 198 was entrusted to a cleric summoned by Basil. The last paragraph, which we omit, refers presumably to political intrigues by the Arians, which Basil's envoy shall expose viva voce *to the Syrian bishop.*

Basil to Eusebius, bishop of Samosata, Letter 198 (375)

After the letter that was delivered to us by the late *officiales* [imperial couriers], we have received only one which had been sent to us thereafter. We did not write much ourselves, because we did not find anyone who could go to you. Yet, in addition to the earlier letters of Your Reverence, which we have received from Samosata, we sent more than four sealed letters to the venerable brother Leontios, the assessor of taxes at Nicaea, and we asked him to transmit them to the house of the venerable brother Sophronios, who will see to it that they be delivered unto you. Since the letters pass through so many hands, it is likely that, either because a messenger was detained by his business, or through another failure, Your Reverence has not received them. We beg you, therefore, to pardon the scarcity of our letters. We should have sent someone of our people, but we did not. That is precisely what you wanted to figure out and to digest! Know then that the winter has been so bad that all the roads were impassable until the days of Pascha, and we had nobody who dared to affront the hardships of the journey; for if our clergy seems to be numerous, they are unprepared for traveling. They are not itinerant businessmen, and are reluctant to live abroad far from home, where most of them practice sedentary crafts from which they draw their daily sustenance. We are sending to Your Piety this brother whom we have called from the country, using his services to carry our letters to Your Holiness. He will explain to you the situation and bring back to us accurately and promptly, God willing, the news from your region. As for the beloved brother Eusebius the Reader [ἀναγνώστης], who has been for a long time eager to meet Your Piety, we retain him here, waiting for the weather to be milder. Now I am not a little concerned, because I fear that his inexperience in traveling may cause him trouble and sickness, for his body is already prone to disease.

GREGORY OF NAZIANZUS TO OLYMPIOS, PROVINCIAL
GOVERNOR, LETTER 126 (382)

. . . I had hoped to meet with you and I was holding, so to speak, this pleasant prospect in my hands, but all of a sudden I was caught by a fit of the illness which had already afflicted me. If a comparison is wanted to describe my condition, it was with me like the squids, which one has to tear from the rocks on the sea shore; they leave part of their arms stuck to the stone, or else tear away pieces of rock. That is how I am. Now what I wanted to beg from Your Excellency, if I had been there, I dare to ask *in absentia*. I have found my "son" Nicoboulos [in reality Gregory's nephew] exhausted from his charge as dispatcher of the couriers and from his functions as postmaster [*praefectus mansionis*]. The man has not too much health and is not used to that kind of work in a remote post. Kindly assign him to some other function of your choice, for he is eager to serve your governorship in everything. But if it is possible, deliver him from his burden.

Notes of Introduction or Recommendation

A number of notes recommending persons in need and charitable institutions have already been given in chapter 6. We add here letter 13 of Gregory of Nazianzus, written toward 365, and letters 103 and 104, written toward the end of his ministry in Constantinople or even shortly after his return to Cappadocia. Letter 103 is addressed to Palladios, in charge of the imperial charities, a close friend of Gregory, who introduces to Palladios a shy young man, an orphan, after a previous note of recommendation had been lost. Letter 104 is addressed to Olympios, governor of Cappadocia, in favor of a widow and her children.

GREGORY OF NAZIANZUS TO AMPHILOCHIOS, THE
FUTURE BISHOP OF ICONIUM, WHO WAS NOT
YET IN HOLY ORDERS. LETTER 13 (365)

I like the words of Theognis [verses 643-644], who praises not the friendship that does not go further than drinking and pleasure, but a friendship that rests on facts. What does he write? "Many are the friends who accompany us around the mixing bowl [κρητῆρι]; but for a serious affair, they make themselves rare!" To be sure we did not mutually associate around mixing bowls, and we have not been much in contact with each other, as we would have preferred, both for ourselves and for the sake of our fathers' mutual friendship; what we ask for is an affection shown by acts. A dispute is at hand, a most serious dispute: our "son" Nikoboulos is in unexpected troubles, on the part of those one would suspect the least. So we beg you to come and help us as soon as possible, to appear at the law suit and defend us if you find that we are being wronged. Anyway do not let the adverse party forestall you, and do not, for a shabby gain, sell your independence which has, I know, been recognized by all.

GREGORY OF NAZIANZUS TO PALLADIOS, LETTER 103 (382)

If somebody asks me, "What is best in this life?" I shall answer, "Friends!" And among them, which ones are to be given preference? I would say: "Those who are good!" "And which ones shall you name first?" "I would not place anyone ahead of you in virtue, I am sure!" I do not write this to flatter Your Lordship but to honor your qualities which we proclaim, omitting nothing as far as it is in our power; we are not only your heralds, but also your fellow combatants, inasmuch as our prayers confer upon you a real power. I wanted to end my letter here. However, since we not only venerate the Divinity, but also implore its favors, do accept— we will not bother you, but merely refresh your memory—do accept this Euphemios who comes as a suppliant. I present him again to you and beg you to receive him with kindness and excuse his shyness; as an orphan he had to attend to the management of his small estate; I would even ask you to urge him instantly, both for our sake and unto the renown of Your Excellency. . . . I beg you to trust in me; Euphemios

182 THE FATHERS SPEAK

is worthy of pity because he is an orphan and because of his character which endears him to me, without speaking of the blood relationship, which binds us both.

GREGORY OF NAZIANZUS TO OLYMPIOS, PROVINCIAL GOVERNOR OF CAPPADOCIA, LETTER 104 (382)

Whatever other favors I have received from you, I know for sure I owe them to your kindness. May God grant you His gifts in return and, among those, to execute the honorable and eminent office of your charge! My request today is not a favor I am begging for, but rather a favor I grant you, if there is no impropriety in saying so. I introduce unto you, through this letter of mine, the pitiful Philomenè, that she may fall prostrate at the feet of Your Justice and shed before you her tears, which break our heart. How much was she injured and by whom, she will tell you. It is not for us to accuse anyone, yet we have to say this: widowhood and the lack of offspring call for the help of all men of right sense, especially those whose wife and children act with surety and make a father act mercifully; it is as men that we do justice unto other men. Excuse us for presenting our request by letter: illness is torturing us!

On the Discipline of Silence and of Laconism in Writing

Gregory of Nazianzus recommends the abstention from "idle talk" praised by Saint Ephrem the Syrian as a salutary Lenten observance. Letters 107, 108, 109, and 111 are deliberately laconic. In the West, Saint Benedict would recommend the discipline of silence at prescribed times of the day to his monks, and Dominicans love to quote an apocryphal slogan of "silence being the father of preachers."

GREGORY OF NAZIANZUS TO KLEDONIOS (NOT IDENTIFIED), LETTER 107 (382)

You ask what our silence means? It means a right balance between talking and being silent, for he who masters it whole shall easily master part of it [by speaking only when it is appropriate]. Moreover, silence makes wise the heart that does not chatter, but spends out only what it contains.

GREGORY OF NAZIANZUS TO KLEDONIOS, LETTER 108 (382)

We do not talk, we observe silence, learning to tell only what is necessary, and training ourselves to conquer the passions. If someone chooses to do this, good! Anyhow, the advantage of being silent is that we need not answer to many.

GREGORY OF NAZIANZUS TO KLEDONIOS, LETTER 109 (382)

I do not forbid you to visit us. If your tongue keeps silent, at least we shall listen with pleasure to what you say, since it is no less honorable to listen than to say what should be said!

GREGORY OF NAZIANZUS TO EUGENIOS, LETTER 111 (382)

Fasting without measure is your philosophy. Mine is the discipline of silence. Let us exchange our particular gifts, and when we meet together, we shall sing to God, offering to Him the fruit of an eloquent silence, as well as of godly words.

GREGORY OF NAZIANZUS TO BASIL, LETTER 245 (written before January 1, 379, Basil's death)

For you he is a mime, for me a pious man. He asked me to write, that he may be liberally received and given audience by you.

GREGORY OF NAZIANZUS TO KELEUSIOS, A CITY OFFICIAL, LETTER 114 (382)

Since you blame my mutism and my boorishness, you who are talkative and urbane, allow me to tell you a fable which is by no means meaningless, so that I may find out whether I am able to check your idle talking: The swallows reproached the swans for their unwillingness to associate with men or to let their song be heard in public, to live in the meadows, on the banks of rivers; to delight in solitude, singing little; and whatever they sing, singing it only among themselves, as if they were ashamed of their melody. "But," said the swallows, "the cities and the humans and their houses are ours, and we chatter all around, recounting our adventures and the ancient tales of Attica: Pandiôn, Athens; Tirea, Thrace; the story of the journey abroad, the kinship, the rape [of Philomela, daughter of Pandiôn, by her brother-in-law], the mutilation, the letter and the legend of Itys, and how from human beings we became birds. The swans could scarcely bear with them, hating their frivolous chatter, and when they deigned to answer, they said to the swallows: "Well, look you. It is because of us that a man decides to withdraw into the solitude, to hear our song, when we open our wings to Zephirus, that the breeze may inspire sweet harmonies; if we sing little, and not before a crowd, the more beautiful it is, for we aim at keeping the right measure in our harmony, and we do not mix noise and music. But you, who settle among men, you exasperate men and when you sing, they turn away. . . . Understand what I mean, and if you find our muteness better than your chatter, stop disparaging our rule of silence, or I will quote a proverb which is both true and concise: "The swans will sing when the jays shut up."

And yet, laconism should not be exaggerated. Gregory and Basil remind their correspondents that they would appreciate receiving "newsletters" now and then and be kept up-to-date on current events.

BASIL TO OLYMPIOS, LETTER 12
(written from the "Solitude")

So far you wrote precious little to us, but now it is not

even little; your brevity progresses in time into complete muteness. Return to your former habit and we will not have to take you to task by letter for your laconism. Even your short letters are marks of your great interest, and we value them highly. Only write!

Basil's letter 21, written from the "Solitude," is addressed to a certain Leontios, a sophist not otherwise identified; it is brimming with irony and sophisticated wit, as can be expected from an ex-Athenian scholar writing to a professional sophist. The "good Julian" on the first line of the missive is of course not the Emperor Julian, but a friend.

BASIL TO LEONTIOS, SOPHIST, LETTER 21
(364-365)

It seems that the good Julian gets something out of the current state of affairs. He too is the object of claims and of numerous charges, for nowadays there are many people who are the target of claimants and are being indicted. Only it is not for arrears of contributions that Julian is indicted, but arrears of letters. How he can be in debt, I don't know. He always sends letters and buries away the answers. Maybe the *quadruplum* is held in honor by you; the Pythagorians have not esteemed the number four as much as the collectors of taxes who exact from the delinquents quadruple fines. The contrary would seem normal, namely that you, a sophist rich in words, should be mortgaged toward payment of the *quadruplum*. But we do not write this because we bear you a grudge. I rather rejoice to hear reproaches from you because, as they say, everything done by nice persons is fine, and even grief and anger befits them. At least it is more pleasant to see one who loves you but is angry, than an enemy who flatters you. So, do not refrain from "unflattering reproaches." Letters, that is what my claim is about, and no news shall be more precious to me or give me more pleasure.

To close the series, two notes of Gregory of Nyssa: letter 9 to Stagirios, and letter 21 to Ablabios. They show forth the same pattern of style: a little story with a tinge of preciosity, which leaves the reader totally in the dark as to the real object of the message—what on earth is the point Gregory wishes to make? Then, in a few lines, he discloses what he is aiming at.

GREGORY OF NYSSA TO STAGIRIOS, A SOPHIST FROM
CAESARAEA, LETTER 9

They say that the jugglers in the theater perform their tricks by borrowing some myth from history or by drawing their subject from ancient collections, transforming it into a real story and putting the entire show, acting and playing, under the eyes of the spectators, as if it had actually happened. They put on the stage the various characters in the guise of actors and mimes; they simulate a city by means of painted curtains over the orchestra, transforming the empty stage to suggest the various scenes. Thus the elements of the story, the discourses of the personages, and the picture of the town on the painted curtains are offered to the spectators as make-believe.

But what do we mean by this preamble? We want to show our little city [Nyssa] not as it actually is, but how it should appear to guests. We wish you would become a frequent resident of our city—we shall see to it that our secluded borough looks really like a city. It will not be a long journey for you, but the favor you will do us is a very great one. We wish to be more considerate to our guests, priding ourselves on your fame rather than on any luster of the entire world.

Letter 21 of Gregory of Nyssa to Ablabios follows the same pattern as letter 9. The addressee has been wrongly identified with bishop Ablabios, on the basis of a most confused manuscript tradition which had not been satisfactorily elucidated until the collation by G. Pasquali. Ablabios, whom Gregory exhorts to a more intense spiritual life, is like Stagirios of letter 9, a sophist, namely a professor of philosophy, desirably but not necessarily a "friend of wisdom." The text of this note, give or take some inconsequential variants, has been credited, erroneously so it seems, to Saint Basil (letter 10), not given. I retain here the reading "Diomedes," versus "Diogenes" (Pasquali), in the second part of Gregory's letter. Diomedes is a hero of the Homeric cycle, who sailed with his companions to small islands of the Adriatic. According to the legend, they were changed into a flock of birds (Ovid, Metamorphoses XIV, 457 ff). The Maurists' interpretation of the letter to Ablabios the bishop as a mild admonition has to be abandoned.

GREGORY OF NYSSA TO ABLABIOS, LETTER 21

The art of hunting doves goes like this: when those who practice this sport have caught one dove, tamed her, and made a pet of her, they anoint her wings with a fragrant oil and turn her loose to join the other doves outside. The sweet smell of the tamed dove lures the entire flight of the wild ones; attracted by the fragrance, they all flock together homing into the house.

But what do I mean to say by this preamble? That having caught your son Basilios and having anointed the wings of his soul with a divine perfume, I send him, new Diomedes, to Your Dignity, in order that you too would alight on the nest which the tamed dove of our story has built. If I see this happen while I live, and if I see Your Nobility raised to a higher degree of spiritual life, I will be in debt to God, to render Him worthy thanksgivings.

On Giving and Soliciting Presents

GREGORY OF NAZIANZUS TO THEODOROS,
BISHOP OF TYANA, LETTER 115 (before Easter 383)

It is also a feast [to receive] letters from you. It is better still that you anticipate the date, and that your eagerness gratifies us on the eve of the feast. That is the fruit of Your Piety; as for us, we give you in return the best we have: prayers. So that you may also have a keepsake from us and our holy Basil, we send you a copy [πυκτίον, properly "a writing tablet"] of Origen's *Philokalia*, which contains selections useful for studious people. Kindly accept it and give us a proof of the profit you can gain from it, with the help of your zeal and the help of the Spirit.

BASIL TO AMPHILOCHIOS, BISHOP OF ICONIUM, LETTER 231 (375)

. . . The book on the Holy Spirit has been written and achieved by us, as you know. But the brethren who are with me have not let me send it as it was written on paper [χάρτῃ]; they said they had instructions from Your Nobility to have it transcribed on parchment [σωματίῳ]. So, in order not to appear transgressing your orders, we have waited until now, and we shall send the book a little later, if only we can find someone to carry it to you. Pray the Lord for us, and be as a gift of God to us and to His Church, through the love for men of the Holy One.

Adamantios, a sophist, presumably an "ex-Athenian," had been begging Gregory of Nazianzus for some profane literature, for which our hierarch had apparently no more use.

GREGORY OF NAZIANZUS TO ADAMANTIOS, LETTER 235

You ask me for books [πυκτία, literally "writing tablets"], and you seem to be still engrossed with rhetoric, whereas we have forsaken it, extending our thoughts higher, through God's grace and for His sake. We had, at some time, to stop playing and stammering puerilities, in order to rise to a higher knowledge and offer our [human] words to the Word, together with the goods we owned formerly. It would be better if you asked me for divine books and not for these; we know that the former would be more advantageous to you and more constructive. But since what is less good has prevailed, you cannot be persuaded; here are the books which you ask from us, insofar as they have escaped the worms and the smoke above which they had been relegated. . . . But let us stop with that joking; it is inappropriate for the present and foreign to our old comradeship. . . . If what we write seems correct, but if you feel that it is unbecoming for a philosopher to take payment for the tablets, just send me the money; the poor will solve your objection!

GREGORY OF NAZIANZUS TO AMPHILOCHIOS,
LETTERS 25 and 26
(before his consecration as bishop of Iconium, 375)

Letter 25

We are not asking for bread from you, nor would one ask for water from the inhabitants of Ostrakinè by the Sea. But if one asks for vegetables from a man of Ozizalaea, vegetables which are so abundant in your parts and so rare in ours, there is little wonder about that, and nothing extraordinary. So kindly send us a load of nice vegetables, or at least what you can, since even small things look great to those in need; and in need we are, all the more because we are going to receive the "great Basil." You have seen him contented and philosophizing; beware, lest you find him hungry and in a bad mood!

Letter 26

How parsimoniously your vegetables came to us! Could it be that they are of gold? Yet your riches are in gardens, brooks, woods, orchards, and your land is "oleripherous" [λαχανηφόρος], like other lands are auriferous; you feed on meadow-greens, but wheat is for you a mythical blessedness and bread is, as they say, angelic bread, hoped for and not assured. So, kindly send us more of your vegetables; otherwise, we will threaten you with keeping our wheat, and then we shall see if it is true that the cicadas feed on dew only.

GREGORY OF NAZIANZUS TO THEKLA, LETTER 57 (372-375)

In the course of last season, a severe frost raged in our parts, and damaged the "eyes" [βλεφαρίδας] which were ready to burst open in our vinyards. Instead they dried up, and dry and empty are our drinking cups. Now, what prompts us to lament over the sterility of our orchards on the tragic mode? It is my wish that you become a vine in bloom, according to Solomon's Song of Songs [2:13], or a trellis laden with fruit; not that you should bring forth grapes, but that you would press the juice of the grapes for those who are thirsty. And who are those thirsty people? The laborers who work at the wall around our church. I have none of our mountain wine to refresh them. I have no other recourse but to your right hand full of grapes; may this fountain overflow toward us! If you hurry, you will relieve many parched throats, and I shall be the first to exult, as I come begging in Attic fashion!

BASIL TO ANTIPATROS, PROVINCIAL GOVERNOR, LETTER 186 (374)

What a beautiful thing, philosophy! Among other qualities it permits everyone to cure himself with an inexpensive food and it makes the same thing good nourishment and sufficient to keep him healthy; for having lost an appetite, as I heard, you found it back with cabbage pickled in vinegar. I could not stand it, because of the proverb and because it reminds me of Dame Poverty, my usual partner. But I am going to change my mind and to laugh at the proverb, seeing that cabbage is a good agent of rejuvenation, which has brought our *arkhôn* back on top. From now on I will hold that nothing can be equal to it, not only the Homeric Lotos, but even the ambrosia, however excellent, which satiated the Olympians.

ANTIPATROS' ANSWER, LETTER 187

"Cabbage twice, 'tis death," says a malicious proverb. But I, who have been asking for it to be served often, I shall die only once, and it would still be the same if I had not asked for a dish of cabbage. Anyway, do not shrink from eating this delicious food, decried without reason by the proverb.

Pascha and the Eucharist

Basil had been consulted by a patrician lady, Kaisaria, on the subject of frequent communion. His answer throws much light on the practice of fourth century Orthodoxy. It belongs to the sole priest, ἱερεὺς, *to consecrate the sacrifice,* θυσία. *Normally, the eucharistic celebration took place four times a week, on the four "liturgical" days, namely on Sunday, Wednesday, Friday, and Saturday. In extraordinary circumstances, such as the absence of the priest, communion could be given to the faithful by a deacon or other altar-minister, from the parcels of the consecrated bread set aside and reserved for communion purposes in the interval between two eucharistic celebrations.*

BASIL TO KAISARIA, A PATRICIAN, ON RECEIVING
COMMUNION, LETTER 93 (ca. 372)

To receive communion even daily and partake of the sacred body and blood of Christ is good and beneficial, for He has said clearly: "He who eats my flesh and drinks my blood has eternal life" [Jn 6:54]. Who would doubt that partaking regularly of life is anything else but living continually? We take communion four times a week [at the altar], on the Sunday, the Wednesday, the Friday [Parasceve], and the Sabbath, and some other days also, when a Saint is memorialized. As for the necessity, in time of persecution, to receive communion from one's own hand in the absence of a priest or of an altar-minister [λειτουργοῦ], it is superfluous to show that this is not aggravating, since a long custom authorizes precisely this. All the monks who live in the "desert," where there is no priest, keep the communion bread in their cells and partake of communion by their own hand. In Alexandria and in Egypt, everyone in the laity used to keep the consecrated bread at home and to partake of it when he wished. Once the sacrifice has been sanctified and offered by the priest, he who receives it whole, partaking of it every day, should believe that he is partaking and receiving it as if it were from the hand of the priest. For even in church the priest gives only a parcel, and he who receives it is permitted to keep it and convey it to his mouth by his own hand. It has therefore the same virtue whether he receives one single parcel from the hand of the priest, or several parcels of the same consecrated *prosphora*.

GREGORY OF NAZIANZUS TO HELLADIOS, BISHOP OF
CAESARAEA AND METROPOLITAN OF CAPPADOCIA,
LETTER 120 (Pascha 382)

. . . The holy day of Pascha has come for us; I know it is an initiation [μυσταγωγία] into the blessings to come, as it is the feast of the Passage [of the Red Sea by the Hebrews]. You did well to remind us of this, both by your presents and your letter. But I have lived through many a Pascha, and it was the advantage of a rather long life. Now, the Pascha I am longing for is a brighter Pascha: to leave the painful and dark Egypt of this life, to be free from the work of clay and bricks which kept us in bondage [Ex 1:14], and to pass over to the Land of Promise [Heb 11:9]. Ask for these in your prayers and pray for us, if you care to do us a very great favor. As for you, may you celebrate many times in your life the paschal feast with the entire Church.

GREGORY OF NAZIANZUS TO PALLADIOS,
LETTER 119 (382)

With Christ I have mortified my tongue while I fasted; now I have joined Him in His Resurrection. The mystery of

my silence is this: as I have offered in sacrifice a spirit renouncing to express itself in words [ἀνεκλάλητον], so also
shall I offer in sacrifice a purified language.

GREGORY OF NAZIANZUS TO AMPHILOCHIOS,
BISHOP OF ICONIUM IN PISIDIA, LETTER 171
(late 382)

We had hardly lifted up our head after the miseries of
illness when we ran toward you, who were the agent of our
recovery, for the tongue of a priest who celebrates the Lord
raises up the sick. Do carry out the best of the sacred rites,
absolve me from the multitude of my sins by taking in hand
the victim risen from the dead. As for me, whether awake
or asleep, I care for you; you are for me an excellent *plec-
trum*, and you have brought into our souls a melodious lyre,
since your many writings have formed our souls to a superior
knowledge. However, most God-fearing friend, do not tire
from praying and interceding for us, every time you cause
the Word [Λόγον] to come down by the virtue of your word
[λόγῳ], every time you divide, without effusion of blood,
the body and the blood of the Master, by the sword of your
voice.

Cult of the Martyrs

*These are notes of invitation to the commemoration of
the forty Martyrs of Sebastaea (Sivas), to whom the memory
of Eupsychios, a recent victim of Emperor Julian (the Apos-
tate, who ruled 361-363), was associated locally. The celebration took place in September; the exact date varies, due
to the hodgepodge of the various calendars in use at the time.
Hierarchs coming to the feast had an occasion for discussing*

the problems of their Churches, without calling a special convocation.

BASIL TO AMPHILOCHIOS, BISHOP OF ICONIUM, LETTER 176 (374)

May Holy God grant you good health and deliverance from all troubles to manage all things as you see fit, and may this letter of ours come into your hand, that our invitation be not in vain, and that you may appear in our city [Caesaraea]. You would add to the solemnity of the annual feast of our Church in honor of the Holy Martyrs. Believe that you who are the most precious and truly longed-for friend, and that our people, who have the experience of many a man, desire the favor of your presence more than of any other, so much are they prompted to love by this short and happy occasion. In order that the Lord be glorified, that the people rejoice, that the Martyrs be honored, and that we, the elders, receive the kind attentions of a true son, kindly come to us without delay, in advance of the feast, that we may be able to talk together and edify ourselves by communicating to each other the graces of the Holy Spirit. The date is the fifth of September. Therefore we beg you to arrive three days earlier, that your presence may enhance the service at the memorial [chapel] of the hospice for the poor [πτωχοτροφείου]. Be in good health and rejoice in the Lord; pray for me, and may you be kept safe and sound, unto me and unto the Church of God, through the grace of the Lord.

BASIL TO AMPHILOCHIOS, BISHOP OF ICONIUM, LETTER 200 (375)

. . . Remember the blessed Martyr Eupsychios and do not wait for a reminder; do not arrive on the very day of the celebration, but rather come in advance; give us this joy, we are still on earth, and in the meantime be strong in the Lord, pray for us, and may you be preserved unto us and unto the Churches of God, by the grace of the Holy One.

BASIL TO AMPHILOCHIOS, BISHOP OF ICONIUM, LETTER 202 (375)

I appreciate very much the opportunity to meet Your Grace, especially for the occasion that brings us together. But my past illness has left traces which do not permit me the slightest traveling, even by coach, to the shrines of the Holy Martyrs [τὰ μαρτυρία]. Almost the same illness did return, and you will have to excuse my absence. If things can be postponed a few days, I will be with you and share your concerns. But if it is urgent, handle the matter at hand, God helping; and count me as one of your members, as if I had really attended the meetings. Be in good health and good spirits, and may you be preserved unto the Churches of God, by the grace of the Holy One.

GREGORY OF NAZIANZUS TO THEODOROS,
BISHOP OF TYANA, LETTER 122
(Date Uncertain)

You are in debt unto us and under obligation of tending the sick, inasmuch as the visitation of sick people is one of the commandments [Mt 25:36; Jm 5:14]. But you are also in debt unto the Holy Martyrs, namely for the annual celebration at your town Arianzus on the twenty-second of Dathousa [an autumnal month of the Cappadocian calendar], at which time quite a lot of business needs to be examined in common. Then do not hesitate and deign to attend; if the journey is tiring, at least the reward is in proportion.

On Marriage, Merry-Making, and . . . Divorce!

Gregory of Nazianzus wrote letter 231 to a certain Eusebius in order to decline, on account of illness, an invitation to the marriage of Euopion, Eusebius' daughter. He seems to have been very fond of the young bride and deplores sincerely not being able to attend. The rite of crowning the bride and groom in the ceremony of marriage, the στεφά-νωσις, distinct from the betrothal, is familiar to all Eastern Christians. In the Greek churches, the crowns are of olive foliage or green twigs; in Slavic usage, of gold or silver. In modern practice, the betrothal and the sacramental marriage are often performed in succession without an interval between the two.

GREGORY OF NAZIANZUS TO EUSEBIUS, LETTER 231
(Date Uncertain)

Time for marriage, and time for building a life, for
our beloved Euopion! And the wishes of the fathers will be
fulfilled. But we are absent, we who more than anyone else
ought to be there and pray with you. I had even promised to
come, and hope sustained my expectation, but making
projects is apt to prove deceitful. Several times I prepared
myself, several times I wavered, and finally I was defeated
by my ill health. So let others call on the Loves ["Ερωτας],
since this childish game fits in a wedding feast! Let them
describe the beauty of the bride, exalt the grace of the
bridegroom, and strew the bridal chamber with speeches as
well as with flowers. As for me, I am going to sing to you
my nuptial poem: The Lord bless you from Zion, make your
marriage [συζυγίαν] harmonious; in short, may they still be
better! This is what I would have wished unto you, had I been
present, and what I wish now! As for the rest, you shall take
care of it and let the father impose the crowns, as he had
wished! For here is what we have decided when we attend
weddings: to the fathers the crowning, to us the prayers—
and prayers, I know, are not prevented by distance.

GREGORY OF NAZIANZUS TO VITALIANOS, LETTER 193
(in Gregory's later years)

I can understand that you reproach me and hold me in
silent reprobation. "We were celebrating," you will say, "the
marriage of Olympias who is also *your* Olympias, a girl of
gold! There was a throng of bishops and you, my noble
friend, you were not there, be it from disdain or be it by

omission." It was neither, O excellent friend, but I think that
a man in a serious role [τραγικῶς] should not play the
comic [κομικῶς], and it would have been out of place and
totally unseasonable for a cripple of both feet to move about
in a wedding feast and become a laughing stock in the midst
of dancers; this being said to joke a little with you, as is
usual in marriage occasions. I am present with you in spirit,
taking part in the feast. I join together the hands of both
spouses and place them in the hand of God, for it is proper
that this union grow into what is best, according to our
common prayers.

*Note 232 contrasts sharply with the warmth of letter
231 on the marriage of Euopion. Gregory writes that he will
not attend the wedding of Dioklis' daughter to a military
man; he had not been invited anyway. He offers his con-
gratulations, urges Dioklis and his company to keep the
rejoicing within the bounds of Christian decency, and warns
them against ribald jocosity.*

GREGORY OF NAZIANZUS TO DIOKLIS, LETTER 232
(Date Uncertain)

We have not been invited to the marriage of our daughter, and yet we shall be present [in spirit] and take part in
the feast. We share your eagerness and wish you what is best.
Now one thing is best: that Christ be present at the wedding
feast, for where Christ is, there also is order, and water is
turned into wine; namely, everything becomes something
better [like at Cana, Jn 2:1-10]. One should not mix together
what ought not to be mixed: bishops and buffoons, praying

202 THE FATHERS SPEAK

and clapping, psalmody and flutes. For in wedding feasts, as in any other circumstance, Christians must be orderly, and orderliness means dignity. This is our wedding present; grant us your docility in exchange. As for your son-in-law, if he conforms to these, you shall have in him a true son; if not, only a soldier.

Gregory, in retirement, writes to his cousin Eulalios, recently installed as bishop of Nazianzus, to report on his examination of a young girl, Alympianè, who is to be consecrated as a virgin.

GREGORY OF NAZIANZUS TO EULALIOS, LETTER 158
(Late 383)

"Truth is stronger than all things" we read from Esdras [1 Esdras 4:35]. The virgin Alympianè, examined by us orally in all rigor [ἀκριβείᾳ] on her personal dispositions, as you had requested us to do, has clearly and freely professed virginity, more than we could have expected, with a constancy greater than her earnestness; I mean that she answered with the eagerness of a virgin and the prudence of a white-haired matron. The strictness of our interrogation appeared finally to have been beneficial, by better revealing the firmness of her resolution. Now that you have been so informed, pray for this child and cultivate the germs of salvation she has received, to the glory of God, ours, and of all the assembly of the God-fearing people.

Adelphios is a young lawyer, established in the region of

Nazianzus and with whom Gregory was friendly at first (cf. letter 205, not given here), but who turned out a profligate and philanderer. Not to be identified with the Adelphios of letter 204, a correspondent of Gregory of Nyssa (see Pasquali, p. 66).

GREGORY OF NAZIANZUS TO ADELPHIOS, LETTER 206
(Gregory's later years)

. . . I still call you "Your Honor" [τίμιος] even though your ways are not honorable. Accept my frankness, for I am moved by my fatherly feelings, and I am unable to delay writing, because of my affection for you. . . . Why do you not listen to what Scripture says: "Leave not thy wealth to women, nor thy soul or thy life to a base concupiscence, εἰς ὑστεροβουλίαν" [Pr 31:3, LXX]. Know this well: You shall regret it before long, when the flesh of your body shall wear out, as it is written [Pr 5:11], and when your spirit, having been pierced as through a cloud, will be able to look toward God and consider only what is good for you. Beware of the trap, do not let yourself be caught by your eyes, and if you have been caught, sober up, lest you confirm the rumor that your mind has been led astray by magic philters, since licentiousness is apt to devise evils. It is painful that an estate like yours, painstakingly put together, be dissipated and ruined so fast, especially in the beginning of a life, when everyone builds up his own reputation, good or bad. And it is much more horrifying yet that you sacrilegiously ravished virgin women, whom your parents and you yourself had consecrated to God, as you told me in confidence. . . . I would have loved to write more pleasant things, but none shall be more useful than what I have written here. I will not write more than this, for I know that if the fear of God does not guide you, words will have little or no effect!

Olympios, in his capacity as provincial governor of Cappadocia, had charged Gregory to inquire both as caretaker of the Church at Nazianzus and as amicus curiae *on the matrimonial status and prospective divorce of the daughter of a certain Verianos. Letter 144 is Gregory's report to the governor. Two conceptions of marriage and divorce confront one another. Olympios has to uphold, pursuant to his office, the contractual nature of matrimony, which governs all the subjects of the empire, Christians or pagans. For Gregory, marriage is primarily the sacrament (μυστήριον) subject only to the ritual and canonical prescriptions of the Church. The letter to Olympios is followed by a note to dissuade Verianos to go on with the divorce of his daughter (Letter 145).*

GREGORY OF NAZIANZUS TO OLYMPIOS, LETTER 144
(382)

Not everywhere is promptness advisable, and that is why I delayed till now my report on the case of the daughter of the excellent Verianos. I wanted to let time straighten up the situation, and also I supposed that you would not easily approve of a divorce. Since you had committed the inquiry to us, and since you know that in this sort of thing, haste and inconsiderateness are to be avoided, I have kept quiet so far and, I think, not without cause! But since time presses and we must report to you our findings, here they are: The young lady seems to be in a double frame of mind, divided between her respect for her parents and her love for the husband. What she says is for the sake of the parents, but as for her heart I do not know if it is not rather for the husband, as her tears show. Of course, you will do what seems good to Your Justice and to God, who guides you in all circumstances. Personally I would recommend to "my son" Verianos to let many things go by and not to consummate the divorce, which is in complete opposition to our laws [viz. Church laws], although Roman law judges otherwise. But justice is to be observed, and we wish you to observe it, both in words and in action.

GREGORY OF NAZIANZUS TO VERIANOS, LETTER 145
(382)

Executioners do not do something extraordinary; they are servants of justice, and the sword by which criminals are put to death is not against the Law. Yet one does not praise the executioner and one does not relish a sword red with blood. Thus we will not allow ourself to become an object of hatred if the divorce is confirmed by us in fact and in word. It is better to be an instrument of union and friendship than of separation and disruption of a life. This seems to have been the idea of our eminent *archôn* when he trusted me with the inquiry in the case of your daughter, because we did not resolve ourselves to remain impassible and hard-hearted in this divorce affair. It is obviously not as auditor but as bishop that he has called me as a mediator in your case. Therefore I pray you to have some regard for my hesitation: if the best party carries the decision, use us as a servant for implementing your resolve—it will be a privilege to be so ordered. But should the worse, less desirable party prevail, look for somebody better fit to that purpose! I am not at leisure, even for the sake of our friendship, though I hold you in the highest esteem, to offend God, to whom I will have to render account for every move and thought. As for your daughter, the full truth will have to be spoken. We shall believe her on the day when, delivered from the fear you inspire in her, she will be able to tell frankly the truth. For the time being, her situation is unfortunate. She makes two parts of her feelings: for you, when she speaks out; for the husband, her tears!

11
Ailments and Deaths

One may have noticed in the preceding chapters the number of letters and notes in which Basil and Gregory of Nazianzus excuse themselves of not being able to visit their correspondents, often high government officials, on account of ill health. Doctors helped little or, among common prescriptions, recommended seasons at the thermal waters of Xanxaris (possibly Kara punar, *the "black springs").*

BASIL TO EUSEBIUS, BISHOP OF SAMOSATA, LETTER 27
(368)

When, through God's grace and with the help of your prayers, I seemed to recover somewhat from illness and to gather up my strength, winter came to confine us at home forcing us to stay put. Although the season happened to be much milder than usual, it was enough, at least for me, to hinder me not only to travel by my own means, but even to peep out of my room. . . .

BASIL TO EUSEBIUS, BISHOP OF SAMOSATA, LETTER 30 (369)

If I were to write down the successive causes that retained me till now, in spite of my desire, from meeting with Your Piety, I would fill up an endless register. A continuous illness, a rigorous winter, and the piling up of business I will omit, for you know it all and it has already been made clear to Your Perfection. The only consolation I had in life was my mother, and I have been deprived of her through my sin. Do not ridicule me because I, a grown man, complain of being an orphan, and forgive that I cannot bear, in the parting of her soul, to realize that none of her godliness is revived in me. Again sickness comes back, and again I lie on my bed, tossing to and fro, my strength almost gone, any hour waiting for the unavoidable end of my life.

BASIL TO THE SAME, LETTER 34 (369-370)

. . . The doctors, I have only too many of them, on account of the sickness that dwells in me, when the pains are unbearable, they imagine no better anesthesia than praying that our souls be made insensible to pain, lest they be crushed by excessive suffering. . . .

In letter 137, Basil apologizes for having been prevented by ill health to appear in person before Antipater, the provincial governor, whose intervention he solicits in favor of a close relative burdened with legal problems.

BASIL TO ANTIPATER, LETTER 137 (373)

It is now, it seems, that I most resent the price I have to pay for being sick. A man of your quality governs our country, and I am forced to be absent for taking care of my body. For a whole month I have been sitting for treatment at the thermal springs, as if I could be helped by it! But it looks as if I were exerting myself for naught, and unto most people it looks like a joke that I seem to ignore the proverb that "heat is no use for the dead." ...

BASIL TO EUSEBIUS, BISHOP OF SAMOSATA, LETTER 138 (373)

What do you think I had in mind when I received the letter of Your Piety? Considering what you exposed in writing, I should have rushed to Syria right away; but considering the bodily weakness that tied me down, I could not possibly rush toward you, unable as I was even to turn on my bed! I had been sick for fifty days when our dear and most zealous brother Elpidios, our "associate in God's service" [συνδιάκονος], arrived. I was all consumed by fever. For lack of matter upon which it might feed, the fever, winding around the dried up flesh of mine as around a burnt wick, resulted in exhaustion and a protracted illness. Thereupon my old plague, the liver, taking over, prevented me from taking nourishment, chased the sleep from mine eyes and held me on the confines of life and death, leaving me just enough life to suffer the discomfort it brought about. That is why I had recourse to the natural hot springs, on some advice from the doctors. But that fierce sickness defeated everything; maybe another would endure it, but if it befalls one unexpectedly, nobody, even if he is of steel, will ever resist. Tortured by it for a long time, I have never been so afflicted as now, because it hinders me from enjoying your true charity [ἀγάπη]. I certainly feel how much I am deprived of such bliss, for last year we were not able to taste, even from the tip of a finger, the most sweet honey of your Church.

Eusebius, bishop of Samosata in Syria, was traversing Cappadocia on his way to Thrace, whereto an order of Emperor Valens had commanded him deported. Gregory of Nazianzus deplores not being able to see him on his passage.

GREGORY OF NAZIANZUS TO EUSEBIUS, LETTER 64
(374)

When Your Piety was passing through our region, I was not even able to peep out of my room, for I was sick to the utmost. What saddened me was not so much the illness which made me fear to be at the extremity, but to be deprived of your holy and precious company. . . .

BASIL TO EUSEBIUS OF SAMOSATA, LETTER 162 (374)

The reasons for which I am not already with you are

not easy to tell, not only because I am hindered by my present weakness, but because I never had the ability to describe an illness so varied and changeable. Only that from the day of Pascha to this day, fever, diarrhea, and abdominal colics, like waves breaking over me, do not let me rise over them. . . .

BASIL TO MELETIOS, ARCH-PHYSICIAN, LETTER 193
(375)

It is not possible for us to flee the hardships of winter like the cranes; and as for predicting the future, maybe we are not worse off than the cranes but for independence of life. We are left behind the birds when it comes to a short flight away from the harassment of winter. First, some hindrance from business weighed my life down. Then, uninterrupted violent fevers have so well mined my body that something thinner than me appeared: and it was I myself! Afterwards, attacks of quartan fever took over more than twenty times. Now I seem to be delivered from the fevers, but I am so weak, for that matter, that I could not hold my own against a spider. This is why all traveling is forbidden to me, and the lightest puff of wind brings about more danger than mighty waves to the seafarers. So we keep snug at home and wait for springtime, if we last till that season, if in the meantime we are not fooled by the disease that has settled in our bowels! If the Lord keeps us in life by His mighty hand, we shall most gladly get to your retreat and most gladly embrace you, our dear head. Only pray that our life be governed profitably to our soul.

Gregory of Nazianzus, mourning the death of his brother Caesarios, a physician of renown in Constantinople, begs Sophronios, a highly placed official, to use his authority for restraining some impudent heirs of Caesarios from grabbing whatever they can of the estate.

GREGORY OF NAZIANZUS TO SOPHRONIOS, LETTER 29
(End of 369)

Not so long ago among other noble persons was your dear Caesarios, my own brother; if I am not prejudiced, he was among the illustrious ones, renowned for his science, before many others the "perfect gentleman," prominent amidst his many friends, ahead of whom he placed yourself and your noble forebears. All his excellence has convinced us. But now it is all over! You may add, on your own, many other qualities to give him honor as by a funeral oration [ἐπιτά-φιον] granting to the departed more than men receive by nature. But do not just cast a glance upon these my words and stay there, tearless; indeed do shed tears, but let these tears achieve something good and useful. Here lies Caesarios, dead, without a friend, abandoned, pitiful, honored with a little myrrh—if at all—and with the poor coverings of the dead—if even he has that much! His enemies, so I understand, fall upon his estate, one here, one there, with full license; some plunder, some are waiting. What impudence, what inhumanity! Nobody to stop them! The most human of those fellows does us just one favor: he appeals to the laws! To tell it in short, we have become a fable unto those people, we who were thought to be happy! Let not all this appear bearable to you; sympathize with us, share our indignation to dead Caesarios; yea, in the name of friendship itself and of all that is dear to you and the object of your hope. Thus you shall show yourself true and faithful to the departed, and you will do a great favor to the living and give them hope. You do not fear it is about moneys we are grieving, do you? What is most intolerable to us in this sad affair is that Caesarios, alone amongst all men, could be thought to have had no friends, he who thought he had so many! Now, such is my request. As for helping us, how, in which way, in which manner, circumstances will show, and your prudence shall decide.

GREGORY OF NAZIANZUS TO GREGORY OF NYSSA, LETTER 76 (Early in 379; Basil had died on the first of January)

It was still reserved to my wretched life to learn of Basil's death and the demise of this holy soul which has left us for the mansions of the Lord after a life-long preparation. And I, among other things, due to my present condition or illness and to my critical state of health, am deprived of embracing his holy remains, of being with you in the frame of mind of a Christian philosopher and of consoling our common friends! As for the spectacle of desolation of his Church [the metropolitan see of Caesaraea], cut off from her glory and devoid of her crown, it is a thing which no sensible man can bear contemplating with his eyes, or hear being told. You seem to have many friends and to hear many consoling words, yet nothing will console you better than yourself and the remembrance of him. To others you have been an example of Christian philosophy and, as it were, of spiritual moderation for better or for worse, since two things are taught by philosophy: treat good fortune with equanimity and bear adversity with grace. This is our message to Your Excellency. But will I find consolation in time or words— safe in your presence and your companionship? May the blessed Saint bequeath these to us in place of everything else, so that, contemplating him in yourself as in a beautiful and clear mirror, we may think that we own him still.

Gregory was mourning the passing of his father, the bishop of Nazianzus (374). Shortly thereafter, Amphilochios junior, a second cousin of Gregory, was recommended as bishop of Iconium, to the dismay of Amphilochios senior, who grieved at the prospect of his son leaving for a distant bishopric and who complained that Gregory had engineered this nomination behind his back. Gregory sets the record straight in a letter of embittered irony.

GREGORY OF NAZIANZUS TO AMPHILOCHIOS THE ELDER, HIS COUSIN, LETTER 63 (374)

You grieve, you weep! Of course I am supposed to be delighted! As you see, I am in a festive mood and pride myself on what is happening! Do you mourn because your son, for his own merits, was taken from you and given honors? You regret that he is no longer with you to take care of your old age and render to you, as is fitting, his good offices? And what about me? Am I not grieved by my father having left us for the last journey from which he shall not return nor show himself to us? Yet we do not accuse you, we do not require from you the consolation which is due to us, because we know that personal bereavements do not leave time to worry about the troubles of others. No one is so affectionate and so much of a "philosopher" that he is able to place himself above whatever disturbs the soul, and to console others when he is himself in need of consolation. But to this blow you add another blow in charging us, so I understand, believing that we have deserted your son who is indeed my "brother," or that we have betrayed him, which is worse. Do you think that we do not realize that all of you, his friends and relatives, have felt a loss? What about me? I have lost more than anyone else, for I had placed in your son the hope of my life; he alone was my supporter, my good adviser, my companion in the practice of devotion. . . . It is on account of earlier afflictions that I was unable to come again to you, because of my mourning and my duty to render to my father the honor due to him—for nothing else can pass before that. My grief was recent and it would have been not only ungodly, but also contrary to all propriety, to play the "philosopher" out of season, beyond what is normal for a human being. And then we thought that the events had outdistanced us and already found their achievement as it seemed good to Him who ordains our fate. And that is that! But now lay aside this grief which seems to me most unreasonable. If you mean something else, let us know, lest we would grieve each other and lest you add to the trouble, much over against Your Nobility, by accusing us instead of accusing others; for we did not do anything wrongly and, to tell the truth, we had to bear the same tyranny, both on the part of common friends and of those whom you regarded only as officious persons.

GREGORY OF NAZIANZUS TO GREGORY OF NYSSA,
LETTER 197 (in the writer's later years)

I had started in haste to go to you and had arrived at Euphemiades [a locality not far from Nazianzus], but I was prevented from taking part in the assembly which you hold in memory of the Holy Martyrs; I could not on account of my sickness, and anyway I would have been importunate by arriving late. I had set out in order both to visit you after so long a time, and also to admire your steadfastness and the philosophy which you show forth—so I hear—in the passing of our saintly and blessed "sister"; your behavior is of a good man and a godly leader who has the knowledge of things divine and human better than none; a man who regards as endurable that which is most distressing to others in similar circumstances, namely to have been united to such a person, and to have let her go to the tomb and to have her placed in the safe mansions like "a sheaf of grain is gathered in due season," to speak as the Divine Scriptures [Jb 5:26], after she has shared in the charms of life but escaped its sad moments, because her life span had been duly measured, before she would have to mourn your death, but after she had received the funeral honors due to saintly persons. I also wish, know it well, to leave this life, if not in the same time as you—that would be much to say—at least right after you. But what shall be our feelings toward that law of God which has prevailed of old and which now bears on *my* Theosebia? I call her "mine," because she has lived according to God, for spiritual kinship excels over blood kinship; Theosebia, the glory of the Church, the jewel of Christ, the pride of our age, the honor of women; Theosebia, most glorious and most illustrious among her excellent brothers; Theosebia, a saint and the wife of a priest [Gregory's wife] equally honored and worthy of the sublime mysteries; Theosebia, whom the age to come shall receive, being placed on the memorial *stelae* of the immortals, in the hearts of all who have known her and of all who shall come later. Do not wonder if I repeat her name often. My delight is in remembering her, the blessed. This is, on our part, an *epitaphion* saying much in a few words and, for you, a word of consolation, as you are able to offer similar consolations to others through your philosophy in all things. As for meeting with you—and do we desire it—we have been prevented for the reasons I told you, but we vow for ourselves, if we are still on earth, that the common end to which we draw near shall not separate us. We shall bear

with all things, for we will not have either to rejoice or to
mourn for a very long time.

*Sakerdos, a priest ordained by Gregory, had died re-
cently. His name is the transcription in Greek letters of the
Latin* sacerdos, *corresponding to* ἱερεύς, πρεσβύτερος.
Thekla is most probably the wife of Sakerdos, his πρεσβυ-
τέρα. *Gregory, addressing Thekla, calls Sakerdos "your
blessed brother." "Brother" and "sister" are often said of
persons who belong in the Christian community, without
being blood relatives.*

GREGORY OF NAZIANZUS TO THEKLA, LETTER 222
(in Gregory's later years)

I was making ready to go to Your Piety, even in the
condition of weakness of my body, wishing to visit you
and also to praise the steadfastness which you show as a
Christian philosopher on the passing of your blessed
brother; about this there is no doubt. But since I was prevented by some circumstances, I have to resort to letters
and philosophize with you briefly on your problems. From
where did the excellent Sakerdos come to us, this noble
assistant to God, now as yesterday? From God! And where
is Sakerdos now? With God, having escaped the jealousy
and the deceits of the evil one, and not without a struggle;
that I know! And from where do we come? Is it not from
where he came? And where do we tend to? Is it not toward
the same Master? May we go to Him with an equal assurance! Worshipers of the same God, we were placed on
earth and from it shall be removed, having suffered a few

ills: a small thing indeed, when compared with the object of our hope, that we may value the reward after whatever we had to endure. The father, mother, and brother who were before us, what were they? A number of praiseworthy travelers! After a little while Thekla will join them, the maid-servant of God, the first fruit of excellent people, who shall tarry a little so as to honor them by her own steadfastness, and to be for many a model of philosophy in these matters. Let us then praise this same power and receive its dispensation, which is loftier than most humans conceive. For the moment, receive this letter instead of our person, and meditate on these reflections, even though you may find better ones by yourself. But if we were judged worthy to see you face to face and to meet with the persons of your circle, our gratefulness to the divine Benefactor would be greater still.

Once allowance is made for the style of fourth century hagiography, the relation of Saint Macrina's death and funeral is a moving testimony to the affection of Saint Gregory of Nyssa for his older sister; as an eyewitness report of such antiquity, it is all the more precious.

GREGORY OF NYSSA, THE DEATH OF SAINT MACRINA
(*Sources Chrétiennes*, vol. 178, Paris, 1971)

. . . She made the sign of the cross on her eyes, her mouth, and her heart. Little by little her tongue, burnt away by the fever, could no longer speak distinctly, her voice weakened, and it is only from the motion of her lips and of her hands that we realized she was praying. Then, at nightfall, someone brought in a lamp; Macrina opened her eyes and looked toward it, indicating she would pray the thanksgiving prayer for the light. ["Glory to Thee who hast shown us the light!" Exclamation of the priest at Sunday Matins.] . . . She raised her hand to cross herself, having finished the prayer, breathed a long, deep sigh, and it was the end of her praying and of her life. . . . After we had prepared her body as well as we could, the deaconess [ἡ διάκονος] said it was not fitting that she should be adorned like a bride in the sight of the maidens [τῶν παρθένων]; "but I have kept a cloak of a dark color [a *ryassa?*] from your mother [Emmelia] and I think it would be proper to cover her with it, for a gaudy garment would not enhance the beauty of holiness." . . . When the day declined, the space all around was not enough to contain the crowd. The bishop of the place [Ibora in Pontus], Araxios—he was there with all his clergy—suggested that the funeral procession should start slowly, seeing that the distance was great and that the crowd slowed down the march. . . . It was like a liturgical procession [μυστικὴ πομπή], the psalms being sung in unison [viz. not antiphonally]. . . . There was a distance of seven or eight stadia from this secluded spot to the church [οἶκος] of the Holy Martyrs, where the bodies of our parents rest.

Epilogue

If the aim of the present essay had been to prove a thesis, it would now be time for me to come to a conclusion, but I had no point to make nor axe to grind. All I wanted was to acquaint readers with the personality of three great Cappadocians: Basil, the stern higoumenos and archbishop of Caesaraea; his friend Gregory of Nazianzus, elevated—reluctantly—to the see of Constantinople; and Gregory of Nyssa, Basil's younger brother, the philosopher and mystic. He had not been born to be an ecclesiastical martinet nor the ideal church leader Basil had wished he would become. Basil always regarded his little brother as an enfant terrible *not to be trusted; he could not forget the affair of the old uncle and some country bishops implicated in deals that smacked of simony, and whom Gregory tried to excuse . . . by means of forged letters! (See above, ch. 6). As a matter of fact, Gregory did not attain his full spiritual stature until after Basil's death.*

The contribution of our three Cappadocians to the development of the Christian dogma was not my primary objective. I have tried rather to enter into the intimate life, day by day as it were, of St Basil, St Gregory of Nazianzus, and St Gregory of Nyssa: the warmth of their affection for one another, their problems in the chaotic situation stirred up by heretics and politicoes courting the favor of the Basileus, their interventions in favor of little people, their foundations for the sick, the poor, the travelers, their spiritual pieces of advice, their Hellenic culture, their Athenian witticisms, the most intimate details of their frugality (cabbages, but not twice a day), and bulletins on their state of health—generally poor! They were giants in the midst of the thinkers and writers of their age; they were also humans, and this humaneness endears them to us as we leaf through their correspondence and their so-called minor works, by no means negligible.

Short of formulating my conclusions in the manner of a lawyer resting his case, I would at this point make the following remarks by way of epilogue. My constant pre-occupation was to gather, out of the writings of our Cappa-docians, those letters and occasional fragments that appeared to me to be characteristic of their personalities. The present book is a sampler; a certain arbitrariness is unavoidable in this type of work; others, with equally good reasons, might have selected other pieces. As it is, let my harvest serve as an invitation to scan the entire field. I am certain that earnest readers will discover, under the catholic unity of the message, the individual traits which make alive and personalize the testimonies of Basil, his brother, and his friend.

This has been for me a labor of love, the contribution of an Orthodox to the history of a much disturbed but forma-tive period of Orthodoxy, and it calls for a doxology. Ortho-doxy is both right thinking and right worship. These are not to be separated, but shall we worship what we do not know? Or, reversing the terms, is not a sincere act of worship the fruit of a genuine faith? Love implies a certain knowledge of its object, but who would be seeking after the Living Truth without the impulse of love? What is being perceived, ever so faintly, by all of us, the Divine Liturgy declares by this exhortation: "Let us love one another, that with one mind we may confess Father, Son, and Holy Spirit, the Trinity, One in Essence and Undivided!"

Table of Excerpts

222

FROM THE LETTERS OF SAINT GREGORY OF NAZIANZUS

FROM THE LETTERS OF SAINT GREGORY OF NYSSA

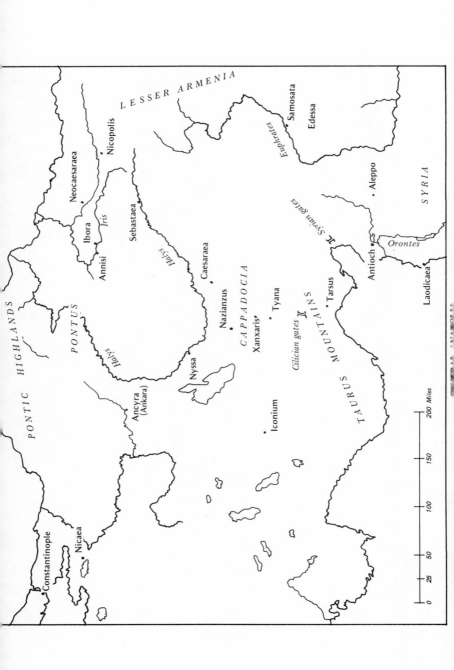

CENTRAL ANATOLIA